Leveraging
Inclusion to
Transform
Your Company

THE
Phoenix
PRINCIPLES

V. Randolph Brown
Janet Butler Reid, Ph.D.

Cover art inspired by
Leon A. Reid, IV and
Michael Vincent McCall Brown

The Phoenix's Journey written by
PJ Forman

Published by New Village Publishing, LLC
12260 Chester Rd., Suite 400
Cincinnati, OH 45246

Soft Cover
ISBN 10: 0-9771761-0-X
ISBN 13: 978-0-9771761-0-6

Hard Cover
ISBN 10: 0-9771761-1-8
ISBN 13: 978-0-9771761-1-3

LCCN: 2005931439

Book production and coordination by Jenkins Group, Inc.
www.bookpublishing.com
Interior design by Linda Powers
Cover design by Global Designs Interactive
300 Red Brook Blvd., Suite 204
Baltimore, MD 21117

Printed in the United States of America
10 09 08 07 06 • 5 4 3 2 1

AUTHORS' DEDICATION

We dedicate this book to those who have helped us grow and transform, those who have provided us with the spirit and energy to write it. This book has been a long-planned "structured renewal."

To the Almighty, known by many names in various cultures and languages

To our families, by blood and love

To our Global Lead partners, associates, and friends

To our clients: past, present, and future

To P.J. Forman, you are the greatest

To every person who embodies the spirit of the phoenix

Our thanks to all of you,

V. Randolph Brown
Janet Butler Reid

For reason, ruling alone, is a force confining;
and passion, unattended, is a flame that burns to its own destruction.

Therefore let your soul exalt your reason to the height of passion,
That it may sing;
And let it direct your passion with reason,
That your passion may live through its own daily resurrection,
And like the phoenix rise above its own ashes.

The Prophet, by Kahlil Gibran

CONTENTS

FOREWORD
by John E. Pepper, Jr.

Retired Chairman and CEO of Procter & Gamble
Current Vice president of Finance and Administration at Yale University

I am confident that those who read this book will benefit tremendously in their practical understanding of how to take advantage of the diversity that exists, how to create more of it, and how to leverage it to their advantage through the process of inclusion. While the principles developed here focus upon diversity and inclusion, they are the same methods required for any significant organizational transformation.

The five interconnected principles the Phoenix character uncovers during his/her journey should be demonstrated every day in companies around the world. Success imperatives for any significant corporate initiative require (1) engaging the Best People, (2) creating a Compelling Purpose, (3) achieving Strategic and Measurable Actions, (4) providing a Solid Infrastructure, and (5) continuous development through Structured Renewal.

The book is written as a narrative that draws the reader in immediately, bringing *The Phoenix Principles* to life in the context of realistic interactions depicting the underlying necessity, the inherent challenges—and the ultimate rewards—of undertaking a diversity/inclusion effort.

In my own journey as a leader, I've learned how ideas, energy, and excellence grow from capitalizing on the insights and capabilities of talented people of varied backgrounds. These are the ***Best People*** to which this book refers. Like every individual, I naturally see the world in a limited way. The essence of leadership is being able to see accurately through the eyes of your team and your customers.

Inclusion should be a strategic business imperative for leaders everywhere. Creating and capitalizing on diversity through the practice of inclusion is not only morally right but also sound practice. Its execution rests on two simple foundations: (1) attracting, retaining, and advancing the best talent to achieve innovation and excellence; and (2) winning in the marketplace as a result of increased understanding and response to customer needs.

The actions we must take to understand and delight our customers are congruent, if not identical, with those needed to understand and help employees reach their full potential. That is why building diversity and leveraging it though inclusion is such an essential strategy. If we're not doing a good job with a certain group of employees, chances are we aren't doing a good job with that same group of consumers—and vice versa.

The vision and growth I have experienced over the past quarter century have fueled a steadily increasing commitment to create an environment and relationships that build on diversity and inclusion. My experience has deepened my awareness of *why* diversity matters and *how* we, as individuals, can make diversity happen and leverage inclusion, thereby reaping benefits for the business as well as for ourselves.

I began to gain an appreciation of the benefits, and the inherent challenges, that can grow from diversity and inclusion when I went to Europe as a general manager of Procter & Gamble's Italian operations. I was living and working with people who spoke different languages, had different ethnic and cultural histories, and had substantially different life experiences from my own. Clearly, we had a very diverse team. As an American among my European colleagues, I was struck by how little we understood of one another. In essence, we did not know how to fully *include* each other so that our diversity could be leveraged to maximize our performance. Then, slowly but surely, out of the need to work together, we began to function as a regional business, with ideas emerging from each of our national subsidiaries. We started to see the power of sharing experiences. We were moving from having a diverse team to having a diverse team that practiced inclusion. We developed better advertising ideas and better products. We saw similar benefits in manufacturing, purchasing, and just about everything else. But it wasn't *words* that accomplished these improvements; it was the *experience* of living and working together. My time in Europe fundamentally changed how I perceived and interacted with people as individuals, and it shaped the way I would lead as I progressed further in the company.

I returned to the United States determined to continue not only capturing the benefits of diversity and the practice of inclusion, but also learning about the challenges of achieving them. When we moved to category management of our business in the United States, I could see that diverse and inclusive category teams—not only in gender, race, and nationality, but also in their functional representation and modes of thinking—had more ideas, more energy, and better bottom-line results. This wasn't some theoretical hypothesis on my part. I was observing it. A diverse group of strong people who were inclusive of each other had a huge advantage compared with a more homogeneous group in any undertaking that depended on creativity and reaching a diverse market.

For an example of **Strategic and Measurable Actions**, I look back over the course of my career and see the particular progress P&G has made in recruiting and utilizing the talents of women. Seeing where we are today, it's hard to believe how recently women assumed major leadership positions at P&G. In 1963, management was essentially an all-male domain, in society at large and at P&G. The progress since then has been tremendous. Women are now presidents of many global businesses. They lead some of our most important brands and customer business development teams.

Women have run our plants in various parts of the world. It's impossible to conceive of P&G achieving the results that it has over the past two decades were it not for the leadership of women. They have, individually and collectively, contributed valuable ideas and insights. And without indulging in overgeneralizations based on gender, they have changed and improved the character of the company's leadership in ways that, while hard to measure, are very real. They include, but are by no means limited to, a deeper sensitivity to the needs of our consumers, many of whom are women.

To build a **Solid Infrastructure** for success, diversity and inclusion must be woven into the very fabric of our existence, both on a personal level and at the corporate level. It is vital for us to understand that diversity includes us all. It embraces inclusion, not exclusion.

In the book I'm currently writing, I stress the fact that *leaders must make diversity happen*. Only the leaders of an organization can provide this "infrastructure for success." To that end, we must avoid the risk of allowing a general pronouncement of the values of diversity to lead us to believe we have accomplished something. We must act on those values to create a general climate of *inclusiveness* by making sure our people realize their roles are essential, that they matter, and that they have an important voice in what counts. We demonstrate the truth of these values in the way we include our people. It can be as simple—yet as important—as intervening if we see one of our team member's proposals being inappropriately discounted.

Leaders must express expectations firmly and repeatedly and then follow up relentlessly. Diversity and inclusion aren't things that you put in place and expect to be self-sustaining. As with any other important initiative, it must hold a priority position in leaders' minds as a strategically vital means to achieve results for which they will be held accountable.

The concept of **Structured Renewal** is one that I now realize was in play throughout my career as I immersed myself in new experiences, learning, perspectives, and ideas. The process of inclusion requires that we are willing to change, grow, and apply new ideas and thoughts. At times that's very difficult and even painful; at other times it's invigorating. In my own journey as a leader, it's been rewarding to see the interconnected principles of diversity, inclusion, and effective leadership played out many times.

All my experiences have made it clear to me that there is no substitute for experiencing diversity and inclusion if we are truly to understand their benefits and be motivated to take action. That is why it's so important that we not just *talk* about diversity and inclusion as if they were some abstract conditions of existence. We must *make them happen* in our own lives, and this needs to deliver measurable results.

Experiencing diversity and inclusion throughout my career did something for me beyond conveying new ideas. It opened my eyes even more to the power of the human spirit to achieve great things despite great challenges. I've seen what people from different, and often disadvantaged, backgrounds have been able to achieve because of their courage, their determination, and their personal commitment to succeed. I've witnessed how others who cared about them and wanted to help them succeed contributed to that success.

Progress in diversity and inclusion will be made from our own acts of courage and belief. It will come as we create advantages from our differences, rather than be separated by them as we establish relationships that show we care, as we support achievement, and as we renew our own spirits. It is through these actions, all within our control, that we and our businesses will benefit from the unique abilities and experiences we have to offer one another. When leaders take action, we take giant steps toward being not only more successful companies but also greater forces for positive change in the world.

People often ask me, "What is the single most positive change you've seen in Procter & Gamble over the course of your career?" My answer is, "The dramatically increased diversity of our employees and the progress we're making on including people in thought generation and decision making." The longer I live, the more I appreciate the benefits of diversity and inclusion—for organizations and for individuals.

This book, *The Phoenix Principles*, allows an individual reader to reflect on his or her own diversity and inclusion journey—or for that matter, any major transformation initiative—in a unique manner. I believe its value is that it's not written in a traditionally academic or business format. It thereby challenges us to think about diversity and inclusion in a personal way and creates a fresh opportunity for furthering individual and organizational growth.

PREFACE

Corporate business needs a rebirth! A renewal! A new beginning! Inside many corporations today exist untapped resources that can dramatically impact profitability. These resources include a virtual army of diverse talent that, if unleashed, could change an entire nation's way of looking at business. Within each employee lives a spirit that can accomplish great things when properly motivated. All too often that spirit is smothered by labels, antiquated rules, fear, insecurity, ignorance, racism, sexism, and a host of other artificial and unproductive behaviors.

At stake is the profitability of corporate enterprise. At risk are the creativity and innovation that can lead us into a new business revolution. Recognizing and valuing diversity and inclusion are truly the impetus that can fan the spark of "potential" into a productive and profitable flame.

Diversity initiatives, however, are at an evolutionary crossroads. Carried out incorrectly, they are a waste of valuable time, resources, and focus—and may, in fact, put your company at greater risk. The time has come for diversity initiatives to evolve into a new, more effective form.

Inclusion is the new and improved approach, a step beyond diversity. Inclusion focuses on appreciating and valuing the inevitable differences among individuals. Furthermore, inclusion involves principles that focus on achieving measurable business results and return on investment. As a viable strategy, inclusion requires getting past guilt, shame, blame, anger, and many other issues that get in the way. Creating an inclusive environment requires going beyond a diversity initiative as "a nice thing to do" or "the right thing to do" and making it a *business priority*. It requires learning from the past and moving into the future. It promises nothing less than individual and corporate transformation. This is because diversity is extremely important—but a diverse workforce is not enough. *Including* different perspectives is central to attaining a business benefit.

The true practice of inclusion releases unlimited potential. It has the capacity to unlock the next great idea, process, or product. It creates an environment where the *best people* with the *best talent* can do their *best work*—productivity in its highest form.

If you are not yet convinced of the need for an inclusive workforce, read the many studies and reports citing data on changing demographics. If this statistical reality doesn't convince you, get out from behind your desk and go visit any of your local stores, restaurants, or other business operations. Unless your neighborhood is totally isolated, you'll see an incredible amount of diversity in your own community. The demographics are changing rapidly. Your ability to understand and implement a strategy based on this reality is a matter of survival for your business. Those who address it effectively will prosper. Those who don't will not—and probably won't be in business long term!

This book is written for those who have read the reports and understand the importance of diversity in the workforce today. We are writing—and working—for those who have the desire to fundamentally improve their corporate environment.

Business institutions are leaders of social change, whether they like it or not. The best cure for many of the social, economic, and political challenges we face today is to increase real opportunities and profits so that everyone can share in the enterprise. *Inclusion* fosters the kind of growth that will ultimately provide more opportunity for everyone.

Most diversity initiatives today can't achieve corporate or social change. Many brave souls have found themselves responsible for leading or supporting these initiatives for a diversity department, a diversity council, or a small team tucked away in some function (usually human resources). Their efforts have been noble and teach important lessons. Until recently, however, these efforts had not been connected to the business agenda and usually fell short.

We've worked to develop a "best practices" model that distills the effective practices of organizations that have developed strong reputations in the area of diversity. *The Phoenix Principles* represents the most recent developments on the subject to date and provides an innovative and viable framework for success for such initiatives. Our experience is based on:

- Twenty-five years of consulting experience.
- Participation in a statistically valid survey on diversity best practices in U.S. business organizations for the National Urban League, entitled *Diversity Practices That Work: The American Worker Speaks.* The survey is based on the quantitative and qualitative data from 5,000 American workers.
- Extensive work with senior-level executives of business organizations worldwide, both large and small, including Fortune 100 and 500 companies.
- Work with fifteen corporate diversity councils over multi-year periods.
- Work with more than 1,000 diversity council members.
- Facilitation of numerous diversity council seminars and presentations during the past twenty years, which resulted in publication of *Diversity Councils That Work.*
- Experience in our own organization with a staff that is "diverse by design," from all areas of human diversity, and who have degrees and expertise in a range of areas, including business management, psychology, organizational development, technology, communications, and natural sciences.

The Phoenix Principles identifies five key elements necessary for a diversity/inclusion initiative to be successful: (1) the Best People, (2) a Compelling Purpose, (3) Strategic and Measurable Actions, (4) a Solid Infrastructure, and (5) Structured Renewal. In fact, by analyzing which of these elements may be missing from an initiative, we can predict and correct certain dysfunctions that will arise.

When a diversity/inclusion initiative is properly staffed, focused, measured, funded, and the team renewed regularly, the company gains insight into the emerging issues around changing demographics and globalization. If embedded into the DNA of corporate culture, inclusion results in better products and services, increased productivity, and increased market share. This book provides a framework to create or successfully restructure your diversity/inclusion initiative *to increase profits*.

Though we've gathered this information specifically with regard to diversity and inclusion, we are confident there is a broader context for its use. We believe the five basic elements of *The Phoenix Principles* are also relevant for corporate change initiatives, leadership challenges, quality initiatives, corporate acquisitions and mergers, reorganizations, team building, or any other organizational strategy or personal development opportunity. The time has come to leverage this information across a full range of disciplines and business challenges. In fact, there is unprecedented opportunity right now to use inclusion to ignite corporate growth.

Imagine your challenge is to lead the development of, or to renew the existing efforts of, your company's diversity/inclusion initiative to *increase your company's profits*. This is your charge. How will you accomplish it? What should you do first? Who will support you? What will frustrate you? What lessons do you think you'll learn?

We firmly believe that *The Phoenix Principles* will answer these questions for you and encourage you to use that brilliant spark of diverse talent unique to you.

INTRODUCTION

This book has been written as a fable because no single, perfect model exists in reality. We're all human, and we live in the real world that is, by its nature, imperfect. *The Phoenix Principles* model is an ideal to which we can aspire. Remember the fable about the sightless team describing an elephant? One feels the tail and says, "We have a long, snakelike animal with a bushy part at the end." Another runs his hands along the belly and says, "No. We have a fat, dry, wrinkled animal, but I agree it has no legs." Restricted by limited perceptions, human beings often have difficulty seeing the entire picture. In *The Phoenix Principles*, we would like to show you the big picture, the complete model.

We will accompany an imaginary character known as Phoenix. You will notice that Phoenix's gender alternates with each chapter. Phoenix could be anyone who has been charged with, belongs to, participates in, supports—or opposes—the idea of any change initiative. Phoenix could be anyone who has been given a seemingly insurmountable business challenge. Also, some of Phoenix's other diversity characteristics (height, weight, age, race, ethnicity) have not been provided. We have left those to your imagination. Phoenix could have any characteristic. Phoenix could be anyone. Phoenix could be *you*.

We also speak of Xine-Ohp International, the organization that employs Phoenix, as a fictitious organization. It could be any company, of any size, in any industry in the world. We invite you to spread the wings of your imagination and travel with Phoenix, inserting the specifics of your own situation.

Phoenix is a talented and committed employee who has been placed on the fast track to the executive level. Phoenix has achieved good results as a leader, but as often happens in real life, his/her personal style is in conflict with the organization's culture and standards. The opportunity to lead the diversity initiative may or may not be a career-enhancing move, but Phoenix eventually learns that s/he must focus on success as the only outcome.

This is a story about a process, which naturally has stumbling blocks and pangs of growth along the way. Progress is organic and not always consistent or linear. Sometimes good things happen rapidly for Phoenix, and then some unexpected challenge impedes progress for a while. Phoenix's mentors advise caution, as we caution you, not to let these unexpected obstacles keep you from staying on track to achieve success.

While Phoenix is a mythical character, the process s/he discovers is not. Phoenix learns about current models for diversity initiatives, gathers some tools that need to be modified, discovers some concepts that can be incorporated into the Phoenix Principles, and focuses on creating a return on investment for Xine-Ohp International. As Phoenix will discover, the five elements of the Phoenix Principles are easy to understand, but applying them is not an easy process. Phoenix's company faces some critical current and emerging issues as a result of rapidly changing demographics, globalization, and changing markets. Phoenix will have to undergo a fundamental rethinking about how diverse talent can be effectively leveraged for the benefit of the shareholders, customers, employees, and communities.

> The mythical phoenix bird is one of the world's best diversity symbols, and its story is universal because it is captured in many languages, cultures, and religions. It is one of the most widely recognized symbols of transformation, struggle, and rebirth.

We hope that by identifying key trends and behaviors of successful diversity initiatives, challenging them to evolve, and weaving them together into a realistic tapestry through our story, you might come away with new insights and ideas.

With all fables, there is a moral to the story; ours is no different. One person can leverage the principles of inclusion into a business strategy that increases the profitability of a company. By implementing the Phoenix Principles, companies can increase market share, gain better insights into the changing marketplace, increase productivity, improve their culture and environment, support diversity, build better community relations, reduce unnecessary risk, and realize their stated goals.

We believe the Phoenix Principles can be applied to every team or organizational situation. This book was written to engage those who are not afraid to imagine and also for those who want a simple "how-to" process.

Now, let's go on the journey with Phoenix and see what we can discover about the triumph of the human spirit. We hope you'll come away with ideas and insights that will enrich your life as well as your work.

Long ago in a far away land, a unique and solitary bird known as the phoenix flew into the forest from the east with the early morning sun. It flapped its jewel-hued wings, scattering feathers among the trees and tinting them with a reflection of its own brilliance. The phoenix lived in this forest for many years, on the highest branch of the tallest tree, until one day it saw flames lick the horizon and a ribbon of gray smoke undulating into the sky at the edge of the forest.

Chapter One

RING OF FIRE

Phoenix sat on the edge of her chair, quietly tapping her foot while her boss, the vice president of operations, administered her performance review. They maintained a wary relationship that had started off with a misunderstanding and hadn't improved much during her assignment in his department. The news wasn't going to be good. She knew it and wished he would get on with it. She was ready for her next rotation in the management program, for something new, and for a different boss. In general, she liked working at Xine-Ohp International. All she wanted was a fair chance to succeed. Outside the window, ominous clouds built on the horizon. Occasionally, thunder rolled, and lightning streaked across the sky.

"I don't know quite how to say this," the VP of operations said. "When we hired you, we expected—" His voice trailed off. He began again. "With two degrees, one in engineering and another in law, the Executive Pipeline Committee saw you as a potentially stellar performer. As you know, our fast track is a process we've designed carefully over the years to give candidates the well-rounded experience they need to make decisions at the executive level. Let's see now." He read something from the file in front of him. "You've been here almost two years. Your first six months in sales were outstanding. You did well in marketing and communications but were considered somewhat unpredictable. Your time with finance was so-so. As a director in operations, you're not showing the promise we expected."

Lightning flashed outside the window and reflected the anger Phoenix felt, which she knew she couldn't show. "I've completed all my projects successfully and on time." The lawyer in her needed to

argue the case, but the VP's closed expression stopped her. She lifted her chin, a defiant gesture, she knew, but she had to rally.

He looked at her with a stern gaze. "There is nothing wrong
with your performance, *per se*. An executive at Xine-Ohp can't
afford to be—well, you're just not as good a "fit" for the program
as we thought you would be."

"I'm not a good fit? What does that mean, exactly, if my performance is good?"

"We don't like surprises, Phoenix. On the surface, you do
exceptional work, but you always leave us guessing."

"I don't understand."

"We've walked you through the program, we've given you
mentors—we don't know what else to do with you."

"If it's just a matter of work style—"

"One of the points of the rotation is that you learn how to present yourself. After assignments to four departments, you don't
seem to have learned that. No matter how exceptional the outcome
of your project is, if no one buys into the process or understands its
importance, it's useless. I realize everyone has strengths and weaknesses. You have to learn where your weaknesses are and find ways
to strengthen those areas. You need to learn from the experts and
draw on the experience of your mentors.

"For example, Xine-Ohp is a company that likes constant communication, among other things. To be successful here, you have to
over communicate—all the time. You must tell us what you're going
to do, how you're going to do it, where the resources will come from,
and you must present a budget and then update us *every* step of the
way on *every* aspect of the project. When the project is finished, you
must tell us what you've done, how you did it, what resources you
used compared to resources allocated, and what return on investment you've provided. You can't drop any of those balls.

"Another thing we value is teamwork. We don't start new projects without running every aspect of it through several department
teams. We don't like to make big mistakes at Xine-Ohp."

To Phoenix, all that processing seemed like nothing but moun-
tains of paperwork. And how could innovation enter the picture if
no one was ever allowed to make mistakes?

"I understand," Phoenix said. She vowed silently to be more in line with the paper trails.

The VP sighed, "I'm not sure you do."

It took her a moment to recover her poise. "I know I'll do better next time. I've formulated—"

The VP held up both hands to stop her. "Phoenix, I'm sure you understand it in your head, but there's something lacking in you that a real leader needs to have here at Xine-Ohp." He looked away for a moment, then back at Phoenix, and made direct, intense eye contact. "The Executive Pipeline Committee has discussed it, and it's my unfortunate duty to tell you that if you're interested in sales as a permanent career, we can recommend you for an independent sales contract. You might consider it. You did very well in that department. You're actually very good at persuading and motivating people. That's a good quality in sales." He paused and cleared his throat. "We're asking you to resign from your position as director. We could transfer you to another department as a manager, but I doubt whether you would want to do that. It would be rather obvious. Or maybe you'd do better somewhere else altogether, somewhere that better fits your work style, as you said."

Phoenix felt the blood drain from her face. She couldn't be hearing correctly. She'd known the review wasn't going to be her best, but her next rotation was supposed to be HR. She knew she would do much better there than in operations.

"You have two weeks to wrap up your projects. I'll have a brief for you by tomorrow on where your work will be reassigned, and I'll expect professional performance from you in working with the team to transition your duties. I promise you we'll be discreet. The story will be that it was your decision to go into business for yourself, or that you found an excellent opportunity elsewhere. You'll receive a severance package, of course. Let me know your decision within a couple of days. In either case, you'll be required to submit to an exit interview with me two weeks from today. Set it up with my assistant on your way out."

He was clearly finished with her. This moment was one of the few times in her life that left Phoenix speechless. She knew she'd have plenty to say later, but right now she just couldn't think of anything that would make any difference. She rose and made her exit.

She passed by the VP's assistant with head high, face burning, ignoring the woman purposely on her way to her cubicle. She'd call later to set up the exit interview. Better yet, there would be no need for an exit interview. By tomorrow she would have thought out her arguments and strategy, and she'd be requesting a hearing. This wasn't a performance issue.

It wasn't going to be that easy, however. The assistant called out to her. Obviously having been instructed beforehand by the VP, she held out a piece of paper with a date and time written on it. Phoenix remained silent but accepted the note.

When Phoenix reached her cubicle, she collected her purse and headed for the elevator. She heard it ding and walked briskly toward it, catching it just as the door was about to close. She nodded briefly to the other occupants and remained stoic during the ride down to the first floor. She had learned early in life to hide her feelings.

She wouldn't come back today. She had some major thinking to do. She drove around in the rain for a while, thinking about her options. When the rain stopped, she bought a hot dog and sat on a damp park bench and thought some more. Occasionally, she jotted a few notes.

Phoenix considered herself a self-made woman. She'd been an orphan passed around among various foster families during her childhood. Though headstrong and stubborn sometimes, she'd learned diplomacy with other children at a very early age and had collected the bargaining skills that were a foundation for her success in business. For the most part, though, in those early years, she'd depended only upon herself. She had rarely asked for anything, but when she did, she prepared a dispassionate analysis of why she should have it with what she considered irrefutable reasoning. Other kids hadn't been able to keep up with her logic or understand her very well, but they sometimes saw the advantage of letting her argue for them. She usually got what she argued for.

Back then adults had tolerated her at best. Eventually a family had adopted her. That home was the first place where she'd received more than cursory interest from adults. Her adoptive family had given her acceptance and love.

Phoenix had been named for a mythical bird by her first foster parents because she had almost died at birth. But she had beaten all the odds and surprised everyone with her will to survive. On her thirteenth birthday, her adoptive father told her a story about a phoenix that represented growth, change, and rebirth. She'd made him repeat the story many times.

He'd been her first mentor, teaching her to believe in her future and inspiring her to be more than she could have imagined alone. While he'd had no money to contribute toward her education, he helped her get some major scholarships and grants. To live up to his expectations, she had studied hard when most of her peers had been busy partying and playing computer games. She couldn't have collected two degrees without him. Unfortunately he hadn't lived long enough to see her receive them.

She wondered what he would say now. The bottom line was that she was being fired from Xine-Ohp International. This was one of the lowest moments in her life. What was she going to do?

There was nothing wrong with being in sales. While not a terribly social person, she enjoyed people. She knew she could do well in the front lines, and sales at Xine-Ohp International could be a lucrative career. But the part of her that relished strategy and more complex interaction really wanted to be in the corporate office. She'd been on the fast track. She'd had plans to go to the very top.

Now what?

She crumbled bread and threw it to park pigeons that seemed not to mind wading through puddles to get to it.

Phoenix sat under the clouds and let the disappointment wash over her. Being fired had not been part of the plan. What was going wrong?

The phoenix sniffed the fragrantly burning cedar and immediately perceived that the time for its next journey had arrived. Many centuries had passed since its last journey, but the phoenix remembered it well.

CHAPTER TWO

ABYSS OR ASCENT?

Phoenix had two mentors at Xine-Ohp, both former bosses—the VP of sales and the VP of marketing and communications—to whom he'd reported during his previous rotations. Both his mentors had been supportive and had taught him a lot, not only when he had been assigned to them, but also during his sojourns in finance and operations. They were well respected and had excellent insights into the company, the culture, and the business. They also had contacts with the Executive Leadership Team, and because of their recommendations to the leadership at Xine-Ohp, he'd gotten a couple of high-profile assignments. Phoenix felt lucky to have these excellent relationships and reciprocated by sharing some technical knowledge. Once he had even provided one of his mentors with an important contact, someone he'd met at a law seminar. He always solicited his mentors' advice on matters of importance. What would they think of this current outrage?

He called the VP of sales, who was uncharacteristically silent as Phoenix related the meeting with the VP of operations and stated his case with well-formulated, logical arguments.

"Phoenix," she said at last, "perhaps he was telling you something it would be wise to pay attention to. Maybe he's trying to tell you something you need to know."

"Couldn't he have told me some other way than firing me?"

"As I understand, you were offered a position as a contract salesperson. You did very well in my department. You could probably come back into management in a very short time. It wouldn't be a bad career, and it would pay well."

Phoenix couldn't believe what he was hearing, but he knew he had to be diplomatic because sales was his mentor's department, after all. "I'll think about it," he promised her, not really meaning it. He didn't intend to sell himself short.

"Phoenix," the VP of sales said, "as you may recall, for the past year I've been telling you to change the way you do things. I knew you were heading into trouble, but you have consistently refused to see it. I didn't think it would come to this, or I would have emphasized the issue more. I'll see that you get that contract sales job if you want it. Please call on me any time."

The VP of marketing and communication was more sympathetic when Phoenix called. "That's awful! I'll talk to the Pipeline Committee. There must be something we can figure out to correct the problem. Though," he hesitated, "I have noticed that since you left my department, you haven't been quite as enthused about what you're doing. You seem to have a serious communication gap with your boss. I thought the situation would be corrected after a while, but it didn't happen. In this assignment you don't seem to be demonstrating the kind of behaviors we look for in candidates for the executive level, but I think they should have given you more of a chance—at least more notice. Keep your spirits up. We'll think of something."

But Phoenix knew he could depend only on himself. After a brief period of self-pity in which he imagined himself as a homeless person wandering the streets and sleeping on the very park bench where he'd fed the pigeons the day before, Phoenix got down to thinking.

Because the rotation in HR was out, he'd have to think of something else. He'd heard through the grapevine a few weeks ago that the company was dividing two of its larger regions into three. The Executive Leadership Team would be assigning a vice president for the new region and would be looking for a director to support the new regional VP. Phoenix thought he would prepare a brief on why he would be excellent for that position and why he should be given the opportunity. He would pretend they'd never said the words "severance package." He shuddered just thinking about it.

Phoenix gathered all the information he could on the regional split. He researched everything he'd heard through the company grapevine and did some research on competitors in the new region.

He prepared his case as thoroughly as if his life depended on it because, for Phoenix, it did. For the most part, he liked working at Xine-Ohp and didn't want to leave. He didn't want a contract sales position no matter how much money was in it.

The afternoon before his exit interview, his boss's administrative assistant called and said Phoenix would be meeting with the senior vice president of operations at the appointed hour instead of with his own boss, the VP. Well, Phoenix concluded, with only a touch of smugness, they've come to their senses. The SVP would not be called out to hand me a severance package. Phoenix knew, too, that the SVP was on the Pipeline Committee.

When he headed for the meeting the next morning, he took his prepared brief with him—just in case. It was filled with new ideas that would maximize his talents. He was ready for the challenge.

Phoenix walked with more of a spring in his step than he'd had the past two weeks. He went through the foyer of the operations department on the third floor and up the elevator to the seventh floor. In the small reception area next to the SVP's office, he greeted her executive assistant.

"Morning," the assistant grumbled.

"Is the SVP ready to see me?"

"She is. Go on in."

Phoenix knocked once and then entered the SVP's office. Seated at her desk, she had her back to him and was looking out the window.

Phoenix wished he had an office with a window instead of a cramped little cubicle. *Some day*. But then a little voice in his head goaded him by saying, *maybe never*. "Good morning," Phoenix said to the SVP.

The SVP turned around slowly, as if reluctant. She gave him a half-smile and then greeted him softly. "Sit down, Phoenix," she said, reviving a little from whatever had been distracting her. She steepled her hands under her chin, elbows resting on the desk. "First of all, I'm meeting with you instead of your VP because he's in the hospital. He had a stroke yesterday. We haven't announced it to the department yet."

"I'm sorry to hear that," Phoenix said, startled. "Is he going to be okay?"

"The doctors believe so. It's hard to say until some time has passed. But he'll be off work for a few months. In the meantime, I've been going over his schedule and have been taking care of some things. I understand you were to meet for an exit interview today."

"No—I mean, yes, that was the plan, but I would like to defend my position."

She seemed surprised but gave him permission, and Phoenix laid out his good ideas and research, and all the reasons why he would be a great director for the new region.

"Actually, that's quite good," she said. "You've done a lot of work on this." Then she asked a simple question. "If, according to what I've been told by your VP, you aren't doing very well in the operations department here at home office, why would I want to assign you to a brand new region?"

Phoenix knew that arguing about his performance quality or saying he had a personality conflict with his boss would be unacceptable. Obviously, his knowledge of the industry and his ideas for the new region hadn't impressed her much.

Then he recalled some other research he'd done a few weeks back. "My next rotation was supposed to be in HR. I have some excellent suggestions for retention strategies." Becoming more enthusiastic as he spoke, Phoenix told her his ideas about recruiting and hiring talent. Also, he had an idea for an employee talent pool that maximized their employee resources.

She listened without comment and then a slow smile spread across her face. "All right," she said, "there is one thing I can do for you. As you may or may not know, the Pipeline Committee is a subcommittee of the Executive Leadership Team that develops new talent for executive level leaders. Taking you off the fast track was a committee decision, so I can't put you back on it, but you seem determined to stay with Xine-Ohp International and prove yourself. I understand you told your boss last month you were ready to be challenged. Okay, I have a challenge for you, Phoenix.

"If, as you say, you are interested in improving the talent pool, our president has been concerned about some potential issues Xine-Ohp is facing. He feels that a diversity initiative is a way to address that. It could be a good project for you. This initiative will start with a diversity council. If I'm not mistaken, this is something Xine-Ohp has tried in the past, but it hasn't been very successful. I'm not sure why."

Phoenix's smile faded. "What—?"

The SVP of operations held up her hand to stop his question. "In fact, the Executive Leadership Team has decided to delegate this task to someone at the director level." She paused for a moment. "I could give you this assignment."

"Me?" Phoenix's brain went numb for a minute. This was not what he'd been expecting to hear. "But—a diversity initiative?"

"This isn't quite the challenge you were hoping for?" The stern look in her eye stopped Phoenix from saying anything. The SVP flattened her hands on the desk in front of her, elbows outward as if she were going to rise, but she didn't. "I believe you have the intelligence and capacity for this project. I understand that many people at Xine-Ohp believe you have the potential to be a good leader. I will tell you that the Pipeline Committee vote was very close. Your record is good, but there are things you need to learn."

"But if I were given a better assignment—an opportunity to—"

"Good leaders don't sit around and wait for opportunities, Phoenix. They make them. Quite frankly, I'm willing to give you this assignment because we just can't spare anyone else. If you want this assignment, it's yours. I need an answer from you."

Phoenix's mind zoomed. Would this be an opportunity to get back on the fast track or a path toward the severance package once again?

"What am I supposed to do with this diversity initiative thing?"

"You know what diversity is, right?"

"I suppose so. Different kinds of people. Different kinds of talent. Equal opportunities for all. Accepting people as they are. Those kinds of things, I guess. I don't really know."

"It includes those things, but I'm sure there's more to it than that. The president wants it, so this isn't something we're going to take lightly. We want a real initiative. This will be a learning experience for us all. It's yours if you want it, but you must say so now."

Phoenix knew it was critical to sound enthusiastic. He must not give her a negative impression of his attitude. "Yes," he said firmly. "I do. I want it."

The SVP gave him a quick little smile that didn't quite engage her whole face. "Okay. Take it and run with it and see what you can do."

"What kind of budget will I have? What other resources?"

She held out her hands palms up. "Why don't you do some research? You seem to be very good at that. Come up with a plan and recommend something."

Phoenix didn't think he could be any more astonished. He knew enough about the way things were done at Xine-Ohp to know that if the project were important, it would be funded from the beginning. Okay, he was being dumped with a project no one else wanted. Diversity initiative! No funding, no resources. Not successful in the past. Doomed to fail again. The SVP's earlier words echoed in his ears, "You have potential … things you need to learn … can't spare anyone else …." He had been fired and then saved by this impossible assignment.

Phoenix realized after a moment that he'd been studying the floor. He raised his head slowly to meet the SVP's eyes. She looked away, toward the window again.

"When do you want me to start?" He realized as soon as he'd said the words it was a stupid question. He had no other duties now.

"Take some time to do the research; get an overview on what you think will be necessary. You'll report directly to me with your recommendations. We want to have something up and running within a few months, so keep that in mind." She turned directly toward him and stood up. "Contact my assistant for an appointment when you have something."

Important projects at Xine-Ohp always had a definite deadline. That was one thing Phoenix knew for sure. "Up and running in a few months?" Phoenix didn't realize he'd spoken aloud until he saw the SVP's face set into a firm expression. She wasn't going to yield anything.

"Oh, and one more thing, Phoenix. When we pitch the plan to the president, if he approves it, it will become a company-wide initiative. I know you're disappointed, but this has much interest from the top leaders at Xine-Ohp. I believe you could make this project into the opportunity you need. And there is another thing you need to understand. I've gone out on a limb to give you this chance.

Yours isn't the only reputation on the line. I expect you to give it all you've got—and more—regardless."

But Phoenix was nothing if not stubborn. No matter how bad he felt about this assignment, he would never, ever let her know. He knew how to research. He'd do it and come back to her with all the information she could ever want. How hard could it be?

That night, as he prepared for bed, Phoenix reflected on the SVP's willingness to give him another chance but only because they "couldn't spare anyone else." That irked him. He pointed his toothbrush toward his reflection in the mirror and said, "You will start up this diversity thing, and it will be the best they've ever seen." But then he realized he didn't really know what was expected. He also recalled something the SVP had said, "... when we pitch this thing to the president ... a company-wide initiative ... yours isn't the only reputation on the line ...." No pressure there, he thought.

The more Phoenix thought about it, the more this diversity thing sounded like a chance to take on the whole company. One of Phoenix's major frustrations at Xine-Ohp was its attitude toward "new-timers." It was a tacit but obvious rule that an associate had to have at least three years of work at Xine-Ohp before "older" management would even pretend to listen to his or her ideas. It would be almost impossible for Phoenix to contribute anything of any consequence for another year or more, especially now that he'd been blacklisted from the fast track. Phoenix and other new-timers had discussed, on occasion, the many fresh, innovative, and potentially significant ideas that had been rejected because new-timers had tried to present them.

Certainly this attitude toward new employees was one of the things Phoenix wanted to change at Xine-Ohp if it were possible. But of course he couldn't change it until he was no longer one of that group. His frustration started to mount again. He reminded himself to take it a step at a time; research was what he had to focus on right now.

It occurred to Phoenix that if this were happening to someone else, it would be a very interesting dilemma. He yawned as he turned out the light. Perhaps after a good night's sleep the situation wouldn't seem so bad. Though it wasn't the opportunity he wanted, at least he had a job.

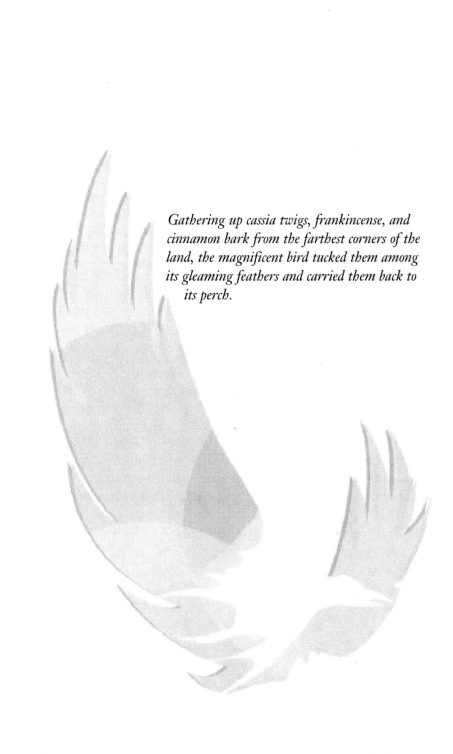

Gathering up cassia twigs, frankincense, and cinnamon bark from the farthest corners of the land, the magnificent bird tucked them among its gleaming feathers and carried them back to its perch.

CHAPTER THREE

GAINING INSIGHT

Phoenix spent her days and a few late nights doing Web searches and reading books and articles on diversity issues. She discovered that there were even magazines devoted to diversity.

She ran across a simple statement that defined diversity as the "similarities and differences among people." While this definition was broad in scope, it was somewhat different from any she'd seen before and seemed contradictory. It was meant to convey the idea that while all people have differences and are therefore diverse, within that diversity exist many shared similarities. The concept was illustrated as a circle separated into six dimensions, which listed various general categories of diversity—societal, occupational, relational, values, mental, and physical. Each dimension listed some specific aspects that could apply to that category. Some seemed obvious, such as age, race, or gender. A person's thinking style, religious affiliation, or work location, for example, was not as obvious. Her "new-timers" dilemma came to mind as a case in point in the occupational dimension. Yes, the more she thought about it, the more she realized that her length of service with Xine-Ohp was an important aspect of diversity for her. Of course, this condition would naturally change over time if she stayed long enough. The individual could change other aspects of diversity—for example, in the relational dimension, if one chose to marry. The societal dimension could change if one chose to change his or her political affiliation. In the physical dimension, some things could not be changed, like race or age.

Phoenix saw the Diversity Circle as an illustration of the way individuals saw the world and interacted with others. When certain dimensions were similar, people often had the same opinions and worked together well. Wherever there were differences, there were more challenges. People had to work harder to understand each other, to find their similarities, and to appreciate their differences. If important dimensions were ignored, situations could become difficult, even explosive.

Phoenix also found an interesting chart that described the differences between legal mandates and diversity, or inclusion, initiatives. She, like her colleagues, had previously lumped all these categories together, not realizing there were significant differences. She thought about several meetings in operations when hiring goals had been discussed. Simply "hiring more minorities" as a way to "handle" diversity had only increased the tensions. Certainly there had been different points of view on the subject, but the discussion had stopped just short of making any sort of decision about what actions were appropriate. At the time, the arguments had been uncomfortable, and Phoenix had been relieved to let them

> DIVERSITY is the full range of human and/or organizational differences and similarities.
>
> INCLUSION is the process of leveraging the power of diversity to achieve a common goal or objective.

die. But now she wondered what might have happened if they had really talked through their anger and fears.

Through various research sources and online searches, Phoenix started to find more and more on the word "inclusion." In many cases inclusion initiatives were spoken of interchangeably with diversity initiatives, but some sources seemed to consider them to be substantially different. According to one definition Phoenix uncovered, "Diversity is a state of being (i.e., gender, race, sexual orientation, thinking style, birth order, job position, etc.). Inclusion, on the other hand, is an action. It is an active process of leveraging the differences to achieve a specific outcome."

Eventually, Phoenix developed her own working definition of diversity. She thought of it as the full range of human or organizational differences. Inclusion she defined as the process of leveraging the power of diversity to achieve a common goal or objective.

As she began to distinguish among various approaches, she saw them as stages of growth, a kind of evolution where actions to meet legal requirements gave way to "diversity initiatives," which in turn evolved into "inclusion as a business initiative." *Inclusion.* That's an interesting word, Phoenix thought. It seemed bursting with potential.

Next, she ran across the concept of affinity groups as a possible diversity initiative. This subject seemed to be substantially more controversial than diversity or inclusion, almost as controversial as legally imposed requirements. The idea was that people with some diversity dimension in common would organize to support their own development within the confines of the company. Certain groups—minorities, women, or those who spoke a native language besides English, for example—might benefit from working together to share thoughts on common issues and things they'd learned about succeeding in the company. The research suggested that affinity groups allowed disgruntled employees to release their anger in a safe environment. The research also indicated that some companies had benefited from the advice these groups provided in many areas, from advertising and marketing to recruitment, retention, and advancement of talent.

After reviewing enough information to make her brain spin, Phoenix reflected on the issues of diversity, inclusion, affinity groups, and legal mandates, and, to her surprise, her reading tripped strong emotions. She thought about some of her beliefs and experiences while growing up. Some were funny, some downright sad, some uplifting, and some difficult. They were as varied as her many experiences with foster homes. At points she felt a bit guilty and other times resentful, but she dismissed these emotions as unproductive.

On the positive side, she thought about her first roommate in college who was of a different race and nationality from Phoenix. This roommate and her friends had looked at life in a totally different way than Phoenix and her own friends. There had definitely been some behavioral and cultural conflicts. A simple greeting or physical gesture could cause a misunderstanding. While Phoenix had thought she was generally a tolerant person, her limits had been stretched by that relationship. After the first semester, Phoenix and her roommate had agreed to be more open to different ways of experiencing life. By the end of their second semester, they had grown familiar enough and comfortable enough to trust each other without reserve. They had agreed to room together the following year. That initial tolerance of differences had grown into acceptance, then into appreciation, and finally into a real friendship.

Some parts of Phoenix's personal diversity journey were easy for her to understand, while others were more difficult. She reviewed the Diversity Circle and found herself trying to prioritize the diversity sections and particular aspects that were most important to her. She realized that other people would certainly choose different areas of importance and would prioritize differently. At different times in her own life, she might have chosen differently, too. Through this process Phoenix came to an important conclusion. How you see diversity is largely based on your own personal lens, which might change over time and with different experiences.

Her research also led her to some information on corporate cultures and group behaviors. Through these readings, she concluded that a company would likely view diversity through its own special lens, just as an individual would.

The more Phoenix learned, the more she realized she needed to increase her knowledge. It was a daunting challenge. Also, Xine-Ohp's corporate culture would require a lot of documentation, which would require her to be very organized. She realized it would be to her benefit to be more tolerant of Xine-Ohp and its culture. With all this in mind, she started a daily journal as well as cross-references for her information files. She was meticulous in her research and methodology because she felt she needed to be absolutely clear about diversity and inclusion if she were to make substantial progress.

She was charged with creating an effective diversity initiative. How would she, one individual, and a new-timer at that, refocus the lens of the entire corporate culture at Xine-Ohp International? Her stomach sank at the thought.

One night when all she had learned seemed to be turning to mush in her head, she recalled her college roommate. In the end they had become close friends and still kept in touch. On impulse, Phoenix jumped out of bed and called her. It had been too long since they'd talked. After catching up with some personal information, Phoenix told her friend about her newest challenge at Xine-Ohp International and the research she'd been doing. The other woman laughed. "If ever there was a great learning moment for diversity, we had it, didn't we?"

"I thought at first we might have been raised on different planets," Phoenix said, and they both laughed. "If only some of our operations units could learn to get along as well as we do, Xine-Ohp could save a lot of time and resources." The thought trailed off as Phoenix again thought about their relationship in some of the terms she'd been studying. The two women had refocused their personal diversity lenses and were much better off for it. It wasn't just tolerance, but the acceptance of and the ability to value each other, that were the keys. She thought about the differences in their personal characteristics in relation to the sections of the Diversity Circle she'd studied. One was a night person, the other a morning person—another source of tension in the old days. One now in business, the other a teacher. Similar in age and education, different nationalities, different races, different religions, different energy levels. Wonderful friends!

Talking to her friend cheered Phoenix. As she went back to bed that night, the challenge at Xine-Ohp did not seem so large. In fact, it beckoned to her. If two individuals could learn to live in harmony by valuing their differences, why couldn't a whole company of individuals? But she couldn't help wondering whether creating a successful diversity initiative was wishful thinking, or whether it might be in the realm of the possible.

When the phoenix had gathered enough spices, it flew to a cliff on the edge of the mountain to bathe in the purest water that flowed from the snow on the mountain peak. As it bathed, it arched its magnificent tail across the sky and scattered iridescent droplets onto the mountainside. Then the phoenix began to sing the song of its journey, a harmony of five notes said to be sweeter and stronger than the song of any bird alive.

CHAPTER FOUR

ORDER FROM CHAOS

Having gained insight into what diversity and inclusion encompass, and his own feelings on those topics, Phoenix felt a little better. Also, now that his files were organized, he could begin to put something together about what a diversity initiative should be.

He was still bothered that he'd received little clear direction from the SVP regarding his role and the expectations for a diversity initiative. So many questions were still unanswered. The uncertainty of the project made Phoenix feel as if he were flying in a deep fog without instruments—a recipe for certain disaster. It occurred to Phoenix to approach his SVP and ask more questions, but she'd told him to do the research and come back to her with the answers. Asking questions the SVP didn't have answers for might be a fatal move. Phoenix thought the SVP didn't have any real interest in the matter anyway. It had been an edict from the president. Could Phoenix go straight to the president with his questions? No, a move like that would not fly in the hierarchical culture at Xine-Ohp.

Phoenix heard some talk that his former boss, the VP of operations who'd had the stroke, was doing fairly well. After some physical therapy he would probably return to his job. Some of his responsibilities had been distributed to others until he was well enough to return. Xine-Ohp was good at taking care of those who had served the company well over a long period of time. This was an aspect of their corporate culture that Phoenix admired.

The problem for Phoenix was that this project had no clear directives. This was a signal to Phoenix that either it wasn't an important assignment or nobody knew what to do. Either way, the burden had now been officially shifted to sit squarely and solely on Phoenix's shoulders. He had to carry the load—alone.

How could he find his way without knowing where he was going? There were no sufficient "how to" diversity initiative guidelines to use as a compass. How was he supposed to direct his approach? Where was it supposed to wind up? What he really needed was the experience of others who had gone before and knew the terrain, so he made a plan to ask people who had been part of diversity initiatives at Xine-Ohp in the past. He would also ask people in other companies what their diversity initiatives were like.

But first, as usual, he sought the advice of his mentors. The vice president of sales was in her office when Phoenix called, and she greeted Phoenix with enthusiasm. "Phoenix, I was just thinking about you. I'm glad you called. First, I want to tell you that you've saved me an immense amount of time with those tips you gave me on how to use my computer more efficiently. I really appreciate that. How did your exit interview go? I really wish you had taken that contract sales position. You would have been awesome. But I heard some other opportunity was being offered. What's going on?"

"Well, that's why I called. I have something I need to ask you about." Then Phoenix gave her a summary of his challenge with the diversity initiative.

"Very interesting. I will tell you this: any project must align with our business goals."

"What does that mean, exactly?" Phoenix asked. "I know what's important to Xine-Ohp, profits and products. But how do I link them to diversity?"

There was a moment of silence on the line before his mentor spoke. "I don't know, but one thing is certain—if any project isn't aligned with our business goals, it will be short lived here. You know we've had diversity initiatives at Xine-Ohp before. They were a great idea, but they just fizzled out after a few months. After all is said and done, if you don't increase sales, no one cares."

Phoenix hung up the phone feeling worse than he had before he'd called his mentor. He had hoped his mentor would help him with this project—at least give him a few answers.

Later in the day, he met in person with his other mentor, the VP of marketing and communications. Phoenix briefed him on his research and the advice the VP of sales had given him. His mentor smiled and said, "Yes, I've heard about this project. I was wondering when you'd show up." This mentor was more people oriented. Phoenix was certain he would have a better idea of what was needed. "I can certainly add to the advice you've already been given."

Phoenix perked up. Finally, some answers.

"In order to align any undertaking with our business goals, you have to know what those goals are. You need to know the industry and where it's headed. You also need to know everything there is to know about Xine-Ohp—where we are today and where we will be tomorrow. Start with what you already know."

"Certainly I know where we are now," Phoenix replied. "I know some of the markets we're trying to penetrate. I know the company's history, of course. I guess I'm a little weak on the longer-term issues. How would I find out? I can't just walk into the president's office and ask that question."

His mentor smiled and lifted his eyebrow slightly. "No, you can't. I doubt you'd get many points for that. Start with some of the other directors who have been around for a while. Branch out from operations, too. Work your way around and up. You may have to go to some of the SVPs eventually or to the president himself, but when you do, you'll need to have enough knowledge to ask the right questions. They'll be impressed by intelligent questions that have a lot of thought and research behind them. I'll tell you what I know, but be advised that there will be other opinions, different from mine. Keep in mind that I'm not your final authority. I just want to help point you in the right direction. Even the Executive Leadership Team and the president often disagree."

Phoenix was totally perplexed by his comments. Who, then, was the final authority, if not the Executive Leadership Team or the president who'd requested a diversity initiative in the first place?

"This is your project, Phoenix. It's your future that's on the line, as I understand from what you've told me. You ultimately have to decide the right questions to ask from your knowledge of what's needed for this project."

His mentor's last remark plummeted him into doubt and low spirits again. Phoenix left his office only slightly more enlightened than when he'd arrived and with both his mentors' messages ringing in his ears, *"You must align your project to the business, or it will be short lived here. You must know our business ... where we are today and where we will be tomorrow."*

Phoenix went back to his cubicle and started his new quest by preparing and organizing a list of important questions that needed to be answered. Now the questions were two pronged. In addition to the answers he needed about diversity initiatives and how to make them work, he also needed answers about the business objectives of Xine-Ohp.

He also put together a list of people he needed to talk to, both internal and external to the company. Once again he could hear his mentor's voice: *"Better to have some knowledge before you ask significant questions."* So, with this advice on Xine-Ohp's culture, Phoenix decided to ask the questions of external sources first. He also sought out some internal people and important stakeholders he thought might be key to the success of the diversity initiative. Still keeping his mentors' advice in mind, Phoenix also considered the order of the interviews. While he wished the formality of the process were not necessary, it was part of Xine-Ohp's culture. Certainly, gaining knowledge at lower levels would help him appear more competent as he climbed the ladder upward in his interviews.

For many days in a row, before shutting down his computer for the night, he visited several Web sites and reviewed current and historical business data, financial reports, and analysts' opinions on industry trends. He searched for information on Xine-Ohp's primary competitors.

Phoenix also found files on Xine-Ohp's server regarding their own policies, procedures, and processes that allowed him to do an internal analysis. He reviewed employee opinion surveys at great length and organized results by various diversity dimensions. He looked at performance and promotion data and processes for recruitment, onboarding, and development.

Next he looked at customer satisfaction statistics, comments, and requests. He took an in-depth look at Xine-Ohp's strategic business plans, promotional strategies, and marketing materials. In the past, he had paid relatively brief attention to this information and only as it related to whatever department he'd been in at the time.

Now he gave the information more consideration and realized that some of it could impact the work of the diversity initiative.

He discussed his findings with others as he interviewed people on his list. Occasionally he added names when he was introduced to new sources.

Soon, Phoenix became knowledgeable about the company's return on investment (ROI) five-year growth plan. He made a point to memorize the numbers so that he could spout them on demand and sound like an expert on Xine-Ohp, its culture, its competitors, and its overall plan for the future. He was certain all this information couldn't help but be an advantage to him.

But he still wasn't sure how to put it all together for a diversity initiative.

In particular, Phoenix began to think about the company's "silos," work groups or departments that functioned independently with few communication bridges to other groups. Intellectually, he had known that other departments made significant contributions to Xine-Ohp's success; now he was beginning to see specifically what these departments did and how they added value. His newfound familiarity also meant he no longer felt so uncomfortable and out of place in other departments. It was a tremendous relief not to have to worry any more about "fitting in." He wished others could have this same sense of familiarity and understanding of the value and function of other departments outside their own.

Through his new awareness, Phoenix saw that while some departments worked together well, others often worked in opposition to each other and made projects harder. Phoenix wondered how they ever got anything done when that happened. He reflected on the many frustrating meetings he'd attended in the past between operations and marketing, operations and finance, and operations and research and development. He'd heard about legendary fights between HR and finance and between legal and marketing. He recalled an informal mentor's advice when he first joined the company: "Whatever you do, don't trust the marketing people." In spite of that, a VP of marketing and communications had agreed to mentor him through a formal program. Now, Phoenix trusted him completely.

Phoenix wondered just how much time Xine-Ohp associates spent defending positions of particular departments or work groups instead of getting any real work done. Xine-Ohp was probably typical of many companies in this way. It was only human nature for individuals or groups to see things from their own perspectives and resist others. If there were only a way to teach his associates what he'd learned: that everyone has something valuable to contribute. Opinions don't have to be discounted or opposed because the reasoning behind them is different from yours.

After a couple of weeks, Phoenix still felt as if he were flying in a fog. He still wondered whether he'd be able to change anything at Xine-Ohp. He didn't sleep at night with any sense of optimism. But the knowledge he was acquiring gave him a sense of having more control.

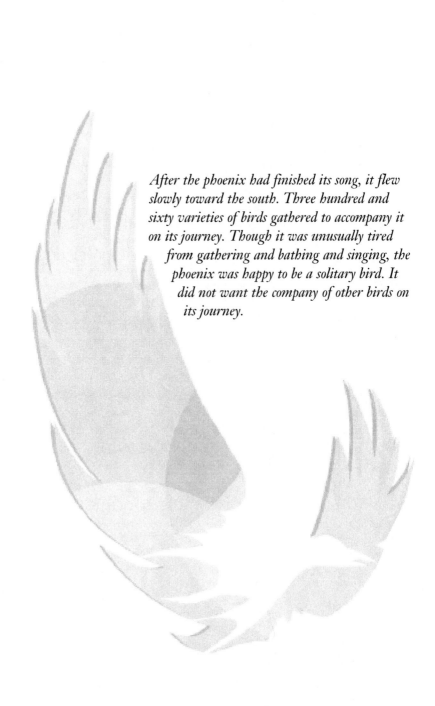

After the phoenix had finished its song, it flew slowly toward the south. Three hundred and sixty varieties of birds gathered to accompany it on its journey. Though it was unusually tired from gathering and bathing and singing, the phoenix was happy to be a solitary bird. It did not want the company of other birds on its journey.

CHAPTER FIVE

TURBULENCE

Now that Phoenix had grounded herself with industry data and Xine-Ohp's long-term business goals and had armed herself with a list of questions to ask, people to ask, and an order in which to ask them, she continued her search for understanding about diversity initiatives and started with other companies. She would try to be objective, to clear out her own perspectives and ideas and let the information speak for itself.

Initially, she received good news—major positive ways in which diversity initiatives had an impact on companies. People bragged about how they were supported. Others gave her copies of tactics charts and summaries of actions that had been accomplished. The good news buoyed her enthusiasm for the project. Maybe implementing the project wouldn't be as difficult as she'd thought.

As the interviews became more in-depth, however, the responses began to take on a "politically correct" feel. As Phoenix probed even more, some interesting dysfunctions emerged. While there were certainly many good things happening, Phoenix was amazed at some of the horror stories. The more she probed, the worse they got. Some diversity initiatives started to look like a late-night talk show host's list of things not to do.

One HR vice president she spoke with on the phone told her, "Our company had several groups going at one time, different ethnic groups and such. They had a lot of meetings and introduced some ethnic food into the cafeteria. I also recall some sort of cultural exhibit in the front hall. That's about it."

That might have been a nice start, Phoenix thought, but limiting the diversity initiative to those activities would not be acceptable at Xine-Ohp. Phoenix's diversity initiative would have to be much more than that.

Her next interview was in the city a couple of miles away. She arranged a lunch meeting with an executive who was about to retire. "It wasn't a good experience. I'd never do that again. You're young, and you have your whole career ahead of you. Don't get involved in it. We had meetings every month. Somebody would start a discussion on some topic that would make everybody all tense and adversarial. When it was clear no one would agree on the subject at hand, the leader cut it short and went on to the next one. Then they argued about that for a while. Eventually people polarized into separate camps according to whose opinions they agreed with. I just got tired of all the strife and tension. And we rehashed the same old stuff at every meeting. Waste of time. *Big* waste of time."

Phoenix called a colleague of hers who now worked in the entertainment industry. "It started out okay," the friend said when Phoenix asked her about her role in her company's diversity initiative, "but after a couple of years, I got tired of it. I had a heavy schedule. The diversity initiative was a minor task on a long list, one that I could drop without too much fallout."

"It couldn't have been very important to your company, then, if you could just drop it like that."

"It wasn't," her colleague said. Phoenix went on to her next call.

"They cut our budget," one general manager of a tool and dye company said. "When money got tight, something had to go."

Another contact told her, "We had some good ideas, but we couldn't get any leadership support. We complained about that. Eventually all we did was complain to each other. It didn't get us anywhere."

Phoenix started to dread her calls. It wasn't all bad news, but mostly she was told different ways to fail. It wasn't what she had wanted to hear.

The cofounder of a manufacturing company told her, "There was one 'hot button' issue everyone wanted to discuss. If someone had a different topic, it just lay there like a dead fish, especially if it was anything constructive or positive. The last time I attended, a few individuals called each other some names I wouldn't repeat in an alley. Eventually we stopped the meetings because of all the complaints."

There was an executive administrator who said, "It seemed like a great opportunity when I was first invited. It was a very exclusive group to join, a real honor to be invited. They discussed social issues with so much passion it almost seemed like a cult. At the end of the meetings, everyone just smiled and waved goodbye, and that was it until the next meeting. The members seemed to be a close-knit group. I never really felt like I fit in. More importantly, they never shared information with or solicited input from the rest of the organization."

"We were determined to improve our hiring practices and turnover rates," an HR executive of a financial institution told her. "Many of the stats we reviewed were highly sensitive. Documents were passed out to council members, most of whom were from the company, but there were some representatives from the community attending that meeting as well. When the president found out that copies of the stats were distributed to those outside the company—well, it wasn't pretty."

"We collected a lot of data," a restaurant chain manager recounted. "We discussed it and formed subcommittees for further study of the data. We kept looking through the data and never acted on anything."

The news wasn't any better from a divisional manager of a large construction company. "One of my direct reports was assigned to a diversity initiative, and the department once hosted a three-day, off-site retreat. The members seemed thrilled about all they learned about diversity. They came back energized and had more meetings. One day I asked my direct report, 'What is your mission? What business objectives have you accomplished?' All I got was a blank stare."

A middle manager in an accounting firm related his story: "Our CEO led the diversity effort with his entire senior leadership team. That team was, shall we say, extremely homogeneous. I was the only person of color on the team. They spent the better part of two hours bombarding me with questions about race. I didn't like it. Eventually the whole initiative fizzled out. There is no question why."

On the other hand, Phoenix found that while many diversity initiatives seem to operate in less than efficient (or downright dysfunctional) manners, and were certainly not consistent with other business practices, there was in fact some very good work that had been done by a few of them. She admired many of the people she talked to in other companies for the things they'd accomplished.

Some of the companies she'd contacted provided her with internal documents, which Phoenix thought were good tools for benchmarking and measuring success.

Phoenix had also collected some favorable research on certain markets, some excellent training and education programs, and some unique recruiting and retention programs. This kind of information would be invaluable for her work going forward.

Overall, Phoenix found, in her research of other firms, a lot of diversity in the types of problems and benefits a diversity initiative could have. Surely the experiences with diversity at Xine-Ohp would not be as bad as some of the horror stories she'd uncovered in other companies. Surely she would uncover some benefits that previous diversity initiatives had provided to Xine-Ohp.

She was wrong.

Many people who had been at Xine-Ohp for many years didn't know a diversity initiative had ever existed at the company. Those who had heard of it talked mostly about its failures. The scope of diversity dysfunction at Xine-Ohp was nearly as wide as some of the others she'd heard about.

Even the range of different ideas and attitudes on diversity, inclusion, affinity groups, and legal guidelines was broad and deep. There were some cases of outright hostility. High levels of passion existed across a wide spectrum, with potentially polarizing differences that Phoenix felt would stop any initiative dead in its tracks were someone foolish enough to initiate one.

In talking with some of the members who previously were a part of the company-led diversity initiative, Phoenix found there was a general consensus that the mission of the initiative was noble, but the implementation was not good, and the impact was nonexistent. Most participants absolutely were *not* interested in repeating the experience.

And yet, when talking to certain demographic groups within the company, Phoenix heard a lot of "politically correct" talk about opportunities at Xine-Ohp. These conversations were too glowing and much less frank. They raised a flag for Phoenix that there was a lot that wasn't being said.

The most significant and alarming fact that Phoenix uncovered was that the last two people who had led diversity initiatives were no longer with the company. Both had been asked to resign. This sent a shiver down Phoenix's spine. No one said it directly, but the intimation was that the diversity initiatives' lack of success had been at least partially responsible.

That's just what I need, Phoenix thought sarcastically. With that in mind, she decided to postpone some of the interviews with senior management at Xine-Ohp until she understood more about the dynamics of a diversity initiative team.

One distinguishing factor regarding diversity initiatives captured her attention. Some companies had established their diversity initiatives by providing infrastructure for them, while initiatives in other companies had existed solely as independent entities. Those initiatives that had some infrastructure functioned far better than those without infrastructure.

Phoenix studied more of the information she'd gathered to understand how diversity initiatives and departments actually functioned. She felt confident there was some underlying principle that could be applied to assure success. Excellent work had been done, often without optimal resources. What might happen if she could set up an efficient process with proper resources at Xine-Ohp?

What most concerned Phoenix, of course, was her own career. Regardless of the number of successful councils and the terrific work that had been done, the ugly fact was that most diversity initiatives were not successful. Her own company's previous diversity experiences had not been favorable. Her two predecessors had lost their jobs trying unsuccessfully to lead the effort. This ominous fact kept Phoenix pacing with worry. Job assignments and rotations were critical success factors at Xine-Ohp. Those who got good assignments were promoted. Those who got poor assignments were demoted or booted. It was just that simple.

Phoenix feared her career might soon be in the hands of an executive search firm. She had a strong feeling that she should be proactive. Just get out now and go somewhere else before she was offered another severance package. With two degrees, she had a powerful educational background. She could find another position quickly. She had a good future ahead of her somewhere. Anyway, even if she made moderate progress with the diversity initiative, what future was in it? How many of the Executive Leadership Team members had diversity initiative chairperson as one of their stated accomplishments?

None.

The phoenix was also a bird of extraordinary sight. Its sharp eyes spied some hunters. One hunter wore a robe embroidered with the colors of the phoenix's feathers. The emperor himself had joined the hunting party. "Oh!" said one of the other birds. "He knows of your flight and has decided that he will hunt you, pluck your gorgeous plumes, partake of your meat, and, thereby, live forever."

CHAPTER SIX

BAILOUT

Several weeks into the process, Phoenix found himself at exactly the same point where he'd started. While he'd done some interesting research, he hadn't even begun to get anything going. He'd been hopeful that his interviews, both internal and external, would help him surface the ideal diversity strategy. He'd been looking for a model, an outline, or a process that he could follow and had found none.

In general, he'd learned that while some diversity initiatives had accomplished good results, they often did more harm than good. Two attempts had been made at Xine-Ohp with inauspicious results. Leading one would surely be a fatal career move.

Furthermore, Phoenix believed the senior leaders expected the project to fail. They had no confidence in him or in the project. The SVP had made it clear she'd assigned Phoenix to this project to give him a last chance and because top management couldn't spare anyone else. Furthermore, while his SVP had said the initiative would get a great deal of attention from the senior leaders, he'd been given no clear direction. The project had no budget and no other resources.

The more he thought about it, the more overwhelmed he felt.

He decided to call one of his mentors again, the VP of marketing and communications—a sympathetic person. He might help Phoenix get out of this crazy assignment. Phoenix felt uncomfortable about bailing. He had run from a few challenges in the past, and the relief of getting out had seldom outlasted his sense of failure. He thought, though, that if ever there was a time for a bailout plan, now was certainly the time.

His mentor listened thoughtfully as Phoenix updated him on the research he'd done, the interviews he'd conducted, and how impossible this assignment really was.

"I detect you're feeling sorry for yourself, Phoenix."

Phoenix was surprised by his mentor's abruptness and candor. "Well—" He paused for a moment. "I'm very good at it. My friends and family have told me so more than a few times."

His mentor laughed aloud. "I'm glad you still have your sense of humor. Let me give you a very important piece of advice. Don't run from this. If you want to succeed at Xine-Ohp, or at any company for that matter, you need to show courage in the face of adversity. Don't give up because things look bad. Show them how it can be done. There will be times when you'll have to cut your losses, but this isn't one of them. Trust me on this."

Trying to keep calm, Phoenix lined up his arguments. "Diversity initiatives are not generally successful. They have failed twice at Xine-Ohp. In fact, there was so much dysfunction around them I don't know why anyone in their right mind would want to do it again! I've gotten no support from the SVP of operations who dumped this in my lap in the first place because the president dumped it on her. It would be an understatement to say that HR hasn't been supportive. There is no procedure, no time line, no budget, no resources of any kind, no clarity of role or purpose. There is no popular support for it either. Most employees, if they even know what it is, don't want anything to do with it. In addition to all that, it's supposedly going to be a highly visible project—but with no leadership support or commitment. It would be best for me to leave it alone."

"Not if you *make* it successful."

"H-how will I do that?" Phoenix stuttered from sheer surprise. Didn't his mentor understand what Phoenix was telling him? Starting a diversity initiative at Xine-Ohp would be like trying to raise something from the dead! Worse than that—it was a monster that would turn on him and destroy him. Why would he even want to try?

"I'm not sure how you'll do it, but I have confidence in you."

"That's not much help." Phoenix knew he sounded sullen. My career is at stake, he thought, and even my mentor doesn't care.

"You don't have to do it alone, Phoenix. Pull together a team of people to help you."

"Nobody wants to touch it," Phoenix argued.

"When you have a feasible idea, you'll get some people onboard. I'll help you do that. Actually, I think you're rather close. Stop thinking about why it won't work and start thinking about how you can *make* it work."

Phoenix put down the phone and tried to do as his mentor advised, but his list of the reasons to abandon a diversity initiative continued to grow. Never had he been involved in a project that had so many obvious negatives. I'll run out of space on my hard drive before I get them all listed, Phoenix thought. He actually had two lists. One was the list of reasons why the project wouldn't succeed, which he would share with anyone who asked. He phrased it in company language around company metrics generally accepted for evaluating a project.

Also, like most people, Phoenix kept a private list to determine his own level of success. It went beyond the formal metrics set by the company to measure a project. The most important reason of all to abandon this project weighed heavily as number one on his private list. He would likely lose his job. And this time, his humiliation would be public because everyone who counted would be watching. He broke out in a cold sweat just thinking about it. Of course, he wouldn't have a job anyway if he didn't do it.

Perhaps it's about time to see the VP of sales again, Phoenix thought. She's very analytical. She'll see reason and give me some substantial advice on how to get out of this assignment. I'll call her first thing tomorrow.

That night, Phoenix mulled it over. He was not a quitter by nature. He thought about challenges he'd faced while growing up when he felt he had to succeed. He always felt good when he'd triumphed over things that others felt were impossible. Why, then, Phoenix thought, am I so afraid of this challenge? Certainly the stakes were higher now than making the soccer team in high school, leading the college's debating team to a national championship, or graduating summa cum laude from a prestigious university. His goals had been high, but he would not have been ruined had he not achieved those things.

Phoenix was fully prepared to run from this challenge. He could not single handedly take on the entire machine of Xine-Ohp's culture. He was older and wiser than he had once been, and he had enough experience now to know that every idea should not be acted upon.

The phoenix was a gentle bird that fed only on air and harmed no other creatures. It seldom concerned itself with human affairs. But the magnificent bird, with its secrets of life and death that even the wisest of holy men had yet to learn, fascinated humans.

CHAPTER SEVEN

THE PHOENIX
PRINCIPLES UNCOVERED

It was clear to Phoenix that the diversity initiative would crash land. Nothing but ashes and charred remains would be left. She also knew that she would have to put in some effort to help others see what a calamity it would be. She would do the work before she talked to the VP of sales.

Her plan was to exit the diversity initiative assignment with dignity and grace, without getting fired again or demoted. She would compile all the information gathered to date and put it into a compelling business overview that would definitively show all the business reasons why the diversity initiative was a bad idea. She would communicate in the detailed manner that her old boss, the VP of operations, had mentioned was the way Xine-Ohp culture accepted information on projects. She would show how much money scratching the plan would save, why it didn't fit with the culture at Xine-Ohp, and what previous initiatives had failed and precisely why. She would show there was nothing to be gained by proceeding. She would share this reasoning with her mentors before she presented it to the SVP.

Just thinking about getting this project off her back made Phoenix happy. In fact, she would be doing the company a favor, wouldn't she? It would save a lot of money and time. Phoenix started to daydream again, anticipating the SVP's relief would be as great as her own. Phoenix imagined that she and the SVP were invited to present this intelligent report to the president. The president was sure to embrace the logic of it and share his appreciation of Phoenix's thinking.

But first, she would have to think of another assignment that so perfectly suited her abilities that they wouldn't see the sense in letting her go as previously planned. The president himself would offer Phoenix this perfect assignment, in which Phoenix could prove herself professionally. It would stretch her abilities and utilize all her best qualities and talents. Eventually she would receive a promotion that would increase her responsibilities even further, accompanied, of course, by a significant raise in salary.

Ah, well, it was just a dream, but it was the best Phoenix had felt in weeks. Although she never held a spark of desire to lead the diversity effort, there was now a bonfire burning inside her for its destruction. It was very energizing.

It was in this frame of mind that she looked over her research again to analyze why most diversity initiatives failed. She found that there was usually no vision, mission, measurements, or expectations. Something so badly organized was bound to fail. Why, then, did some initiatives succeed in spite of all these negative factors?

As she read over her materials, Phoenix was intrigued about potentially bringing together people with diverse backgrounds and experiences to address pertinent business opportunities. Wouldn't it be great if it could work? She was becoming peeved that no real thought had been given to the diversity initiative process by Xine-Ohp.

In this irritated frame of mind, she called her mentor, the VP of sales.

"You're going to scrap the diversity initiative?" her mentor asked, surprised. "You don't have the authority to do that."

"I'm preparing a comprehensive analysis to show that diversity initiatives are not treated with the same rigor and thought processes as other business initiatives."

"Okay." Her mentor was silent for a moment. Phoenix could hear her tapping the desk with her fingers. "If you're going to recommend tanking the diversity initiative, I must warn you that you'll need some very convincing arguments. You know how things are at Xine-Ohp. Even if something isn't really supported, our corporate culture is to challenge everything—even a decision not to do something no one wants to do anyway. When you meet with the SVP, she will ask you some very challenging questions."

"Yes, I'm prepared for that," Phoenix replied confidently. "I didn't say a diversity initiative isn't a good idea. I'm only saying it won't work at Xine-Ohp."

"What if you could make it work? Wouldn't that be phenomenal?"

Now she was starting to sound like the VP of marketing and communications. Phoenix wondered whether the two of them had discussed this behind her back. Or had she glimpsed Phoenix's own thoughts?

"Certainly there are areas where a diversity initiative could help the company. It's just that—"

"Tell me some."

"Well, as a result of changing demographics and increased minority populations, we need to be conscious of minority spending habits and practices. Age, gender, and regional preferences are important, too. You were talking about market share—understanding these markets better and the consumers within them could help increase market share with some of our products. Better control of risk is another—lawsuits. As you said, we need to know how to manage diverse groups of employees and customers. And I believe we could improve innovation by recruiting more diverse talent. We could reduce turnover costs by learning what it takes to retain associates. Improved communications with cross-functional teams would make them more effective. These kinds of things increase efficiency and give us a chance to create more innovative products. Community relations are becoming very important in today's economy, as well."

"That sounds good, Phoenix. You've really done your homework."

"Thank you. I think. I'm not sure whether you're supporting me in ditching the project or talking me into going forward with it."

"I don't know. Maybe you ought to think about it more. Perhaps the benefits would outweigh the problems you'd have to overcome."

Phoenix began to fume. "I have been given no budget, no staff, and no resources. How can I go forward with a project like that?"

"Why were they denied to you?"

"Denied? Well, they weren't denied. Not exactly."

"What was your recommendation, then?"

"There was no recommendation. I didn't see any point in recommending anything for a project that is doomed to fail anyway. I am recommending the project be scrapped," Phoenix reminded her mentor.

"What is required for success that you find lacking?"

"First, I need some other people to work on the project. I have tons of data on how not having enough people or the best people for the job had a negative impact on the outcome of diversity initiatives. It seems especially important because of the deep emotions often attached to diversity topics."

"Having the best people you can get is the nucleus for any kind of work."

"The *best* people," Phoenix repeated.

"Yes, certainly. Write that down. It'll help organize your thoughts."

Phoenix opened a new page in her computer program and typed *the best people*.

"What else?" her mentor asked.

"In reviewing other diversity initiatives, the lack of purpose—that is, a compelling vision and mission with a strategic link to the company's overall business objectives—caused many initiatives to fail. In other projects I've worked on, when there was a clear and compelling set of business objectives and a well-thought-out strategic plan, there was movement."

"That reminds me of what I told you a few weeks ago, remember?"

"Yes, I do remember. You said, 'Whatever you do must be aligned with the business, or it will be short lived here.' And then I asked you how Xine-Ohp's profits and products could be tied to a diversity initiative," Phoenix reminded her.

"Well, that's the problem, isn't it? Okay, you need a compelling purpose."

Phoenix typed *compelling purpose* just under *best people*.

"What else?"

Phoenix thought about it a few seconds before answering. "Some diversity initiatives have achieved good results; however, much of the work was not considered strategic or measurable. This was the one area where I collected some excellent information and resources. All business initiatives have to prove a result or generate some form of return on investment. Any teams I've worked with in the past had to have some objective toward that end. You know— win the game, get more sales, fix a problem, beat someone else, do it faster, increase quality."

"So, any actions taken as a result of the diversity initiative must be part of a strategic plan, aligned with the mission and vision that are spelled out in your compelling purpose. And, those strategic actions must lead to results that can be measured."

"Yes," Phoenix said and typed *strategic and measurable actions*.

"What else does this initiative lack that's going to make it fail?"

This is great, Phoenix thought. She said, "Thank you so much for helping me with this."

"Think nothing of it. That's what mentors do. Keep going."

"When I think about the other diversity initiatives in Xine-Ohp's previous experience, they really didn't have any sort of budget or other resources. There was no support from the leadership. There also didn't seem to be any good method of communication. These are the things I've been mostly concerned about from the beginning. They're all things I think of as essential infrastructure. In the past, there was no consistent and adequate support from the company and its resources to build a solid infrastructure."

"That sounds reasonable."

Solid infrastructure was added to Phoenix's list. Phoenix now had four basic things she believed would be necessary for a successful diversity initiative. Certainly they were things any functioning team or project would need to be successful.

"Okay, what else?" asked her mentor.

"Something else is missing, but I'm not sure what it is. You know, I remember some conversations I had during my interviews," Phoenix said. "Some diversity initiatives started out well but then somehow lost their energy. They became stagnant and dull after a while."

"So there is a need for renewed enthusiasm."

"Yes. Diversity initiatives seemed to be unique in this way. Or maybe not. Maybe they just need more of what any group or individual would need to keep enthusiasm high. Education and development of the members. Reinvention of the process. An influx of new ideas. Renewed energy." This requirement, Phoenix thought, is actually the essence of leveraging and practicing the principles of diversity. "This kind of renewal would have to occur constantly, not just arbitrarily whenever they felt like it or had a few extra dollars in the budget."

"Renewal would have to be part of the structure of the team."

Phoenix realized how true it was as soon as her mentor said it. "Yes. Exactly."

She typed *structured renewal* beneath the others.

"What else?"

Phoenix read the list. "The best people, compelling purpose, strategic and measurable actions, solid infrastructure, and structured renewal. I can't think of anything else."

"So these are the things that are missing in your current project?"

"Yes."

"Would the project have a chance if you were given the people and the resources and if you could find a way to tie it to the business objectives?"

"Yes. Possibly."

"You said earlier that you hadn't been given any resources, but you haven't been denied any either, is that right?"

"When you put it that way—"

"I would say you're quite lucky. One could say you've been given a blank slate. How often does that happen? Not often, I can tell you."

"You don't understand—"

"Maybe your thought processes are backward," her mentor suggested. "Turn the situation around and ask, 'What might happen if I had all that I need?' Don't think about the *difficulty* of getting it. Just think of *getting* it. You know, the SVP asked you for recommendations. You could give her these five requirements and recommend an allocation of resources."

Phoenix was in a daze when she hung up the phone. Her five requirements had originally been meant to serve as an argument to destroy the diversity initiative idea. But now they were the framework for a successful diversity initiative. As she contemplated them, she realized they were more than requirements for a diversity initiative. They could be applicable to team development or organizational transformation. Taking the requirements a step further, they could, perhaps, transform the lives of individuals as well. Perhaps she had uncovered some fundamental laws that defined success in general.

Phoenix was still a bit puzzled though. She considered her early discoveries about diversity, affinity groups, and legal mandates. There just seemed to be so much angst about them. All were important concepts, but they might not be effective at Xine-Ohp.

Many companies needed diversity initiatives to increase diversity in their workforce, but Xine-Ohp hired a lot of people with a wide range of talents and backgrounds. It was a multinational corporation, after all. Because Xine-Ohp was already diverse, Phoenix knew their diversity initiative would need a different focus. Its focus would have to center on using existing diversity for the benefit of the company.

As she mulled it over, she recalled the word "inclusion." She looked through some of her original research files for some documents on inclusion. The concept, while it hinged on diversity, was considered quite different from diversity. Inclusion was an evolutionary step beyond diversity, which leveraged the wealth of diverse talents, thought processes, and cultural traditions of all kinds to benefit the corporation. Diversity had to do with describing similarities and differences. Inclusion was a *process* that allowed varied voices to be heard and acted upon to get results that would increase the profitability of the company's products.

Inclusion, then, could be a great "fit" for Xine-Ohp. If it could be significantly aligned with the ROI five-year growth plan, inclusion could bring with it a new source of energy and perspective on the business.

Phoenix thought about how she could use the information she'd discovered in her research to bring the benefits of inclusion to the organization. She listed again her five necessary ingredients for a successful team: bringing *the best people* together, having a *compelling purpose* to focus action, achieving results through *strategic and measurable actions*, aligning and integrating with the norms of Xine-Ohp's culture to have a *solid infrastructure*, and staying dynamic and strong through *structured renewal*.

She had started the conversation with her mentor to kill the diversity idea and create a plan to exit the project diplomatically—

and without losing her job in the process. Now she had identified a basic strategy for success, a process composed of five elements needed for highly functioning teams. A new and potentially viable process had emerged from what she had thought was impossible.

Phoenix wondered whether her mentor could be right. Perhaps, like the mythical phoenix bird rising with renewed life from its own ashes, something new could arise out of the ashes of previous diversity work at Xine-Ohp.

Phoenix was extremely pleased with the idea. She tried to think of a descriptive name to summarize the components of her new process. Privately, she thought of them as the Phoenix Principles.

THE PHOENIX PRINCIPLES

The Best People
Compelling Purpose
Strategic and Measurable Actions
Solid Infrastructure
Structured Renewal

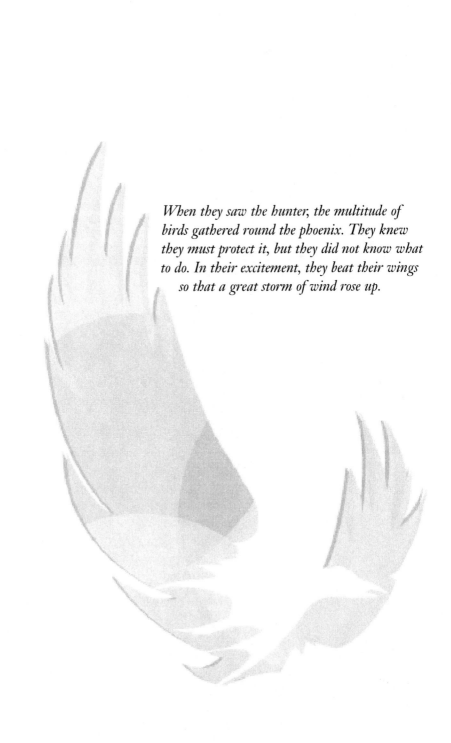

When they saw the hunter, the multitude of birds gathered round the phoenix. They knew they must protect it, but they did not know what to do. In their excitement, they beat their wings so that a great storm of wind rose up.

CHAPTER EIGHT

A FORK IN THE ROAD

Even though Phoenix had identified inclusion as the process that fit Xine-Ohp, and had outlined the elements of that process, which he privately called the Phoenix Principles, he had doubts about whether he would be able to overcome the *new-timer* label in order to implement them. Seniority was a strong inclusion issue at Xine-Ohp.

For a moment he felt a flash of strong conviction that Xine-Ohp needed inclusion. What was the magic of the three-year mark? He was an intelligent person. His ideas were as good as anyone's. The barrier against the new-timer was a worthy challenge. But then the enormity of the job overwhelmed him, and he began to lose confidence. As far as he knew, this custom had never been challenged. He felt another flood of self-pity.

He needed more help. His mentors had been invaluable in getting him this far, so he decided to invite them both to lunch to discuss the matter further. He knew his mentors would not approve a defeatist attitude, so he tried to harbor only positive thoughts. Perhaps the three of them together could come up with some strategy on what to do.

He called the VP of sales and invited her to lunch.

"Are you buying?" she teased.

"Of course," Phoenix said. When he called the VP of marketing and communications, he accepted as well.

It was an interesting situation for Phoenix. He'd never met with both his mentors at the same time before. After some initial small talk and after the waiter had taken their orders, they jumped into the purpose of their meeting. "When I called you the other day, I was seeking your advice on the best way to exit the project. But I knew you would be disappointed in me if I quit. With your help," Phoenix caught a look in the eye of the VP of sales, "I've actually created some principles essential to the success of the inclusion initiative, or perhaps any team or project."

His mentors listened intently. Their enthusiasm showed in their expressions. They beamed smiles at him. Their eyes were intense. The food went untouched.

Phoenix then reviewed the five success elements, or what he privately referred to as the Phoenix Principles: Best People, Compelling Purpose, Solid Infrastructure, Strategic and Measurable Actions, and Structured Renewal.

He explained the principle of inclusion as a process that allowed the voices of diverse groups of associates to be heard and acted upon to increase the profitability of the company. "And, as you know," he said, "it will be critical to focus on products, profits, and return on investment. These will be essential in bringing the process to life."

Phoenix could see that his mentors were pleased with his concepts. In the glow of their approval, he couldn't help being very pleased with himself.

Then, almost in unison, they asked Phoenix, "So what do you plan to do with this information?"

"I was hoping you might help me with that."

"I sense you're still hesitant to go forward with it," said the VP of marketing and communications.

"Yes, I am."

"Certainly it's a critical decision," said the VP of sales. "You're the only one who can make it."

"The main thing," the VP of marketing and communications added, "is that whatever decision you make, you must be fully committed."

"Absolutely," said the VP of sales.

"Commitment and competence are the two determining factors for an individual's success," the VP of marketing and communications added.

The VP of sales concurred. "There is no question about your competence, Phoenix. I think everyone recognizes that."

"I don't know. I doubt whether the VP and SVP of operations would agree with that." Phoenix noticed a look of frustration that passed between his two mentors.

The VP of marketing and communications recovered first. She smiled enigmatically. "That may or may not be, Phoenix. It's not for us to say what's in someone else's mind. But right now, it's your commitment that's in question. That's the bigger issue."

The VP of sales jumped in. "Leadership effectiveness is generally presented in three distinct ways—in your thinking, through passion and commitment, and through your actions. What you've done so far is a good academic exercise. That is, you've done the thinking part, but you haven't really put your heart into it. And you'll never know success until you take some actions to put your goals into place. Should you decide to move forward with the project, your real challenge won't be on paper, but with thinking, feeling people who live in a world of actions."

"Try not to make commitment dependent on your confidence level, Phoenix," the VP of marketing and communications said. "Confidence will come later if you're fully committed to the project. As our VP of sales told you, you've done the thinking part. Now what I'd like to know is: *Do you feel this initiative is right for Xine-Ohp?*"

"Yes, if—"

"Don't qualify your answer. Either it is or it isn't."

"Yes, I suppose."

He sighed and held Phoenix's gaze with a long-suffering look.

"Yes," Phoenix said meekly.

"Do you truly feel your process is sound?"

"Yes, but—"

Phoenix's mentor lowered his eyebrows.

"Yes."

Phoenix knew his mentors were right. He did have sound principles. "Now let's think about the commitment part. Why do you feel unprepared to take on this challenge?"

Phoenix thought for a moment. "The diversity initiative is a low-priority project. I'm a *new-timer*. There is no support from the ranks or from the leaders. I honestly don't feel I should waste my time on it." Phoenix felt his face flush as the anger bubbled to the surface again. "I have a lot to offer this company. I could do justice to a decent project."

"The project isn't worthy of you. Is that what you're saying?"

Phoenix's irritation was beginning to spread toward the VP of marketing and communications. "I wouldn't put it quite that way, but if you insist, yes. A project like this is not worthy of everything I've put into my career." That hadn't come out quite the way Phoenix intended. He had to explain it further. "In general terms, inclusion is a worthy ideal, but Xine-Ohp doesn't accept it as such. In that way, it is not worthy of me. And I resent being put in this position. I don't deserve it."

The eyebrows lowered again.

"All right. I know. Life isn't about what you deserve. I've been told that before," Phoenix confessed.

"Is it safe to say that you don't want to go forward with the project or that you are still undecided?" the VP of sales asked.

Phoenix realized that as much as he had enjoyed creating the Phoenix Principles and discovering the inclusion process, he was still stuck at a fork in the road, not knowing which way to go.

The VP of sales cleared her throat. "Let's analyze it a bit further. Let's just lay out the good, the bad, and the ugly. Then, Phoenix, you need to make a decision and act on it, one way or another. The worst thing you can do is let yourself be hung up on it any longer."

"You're right," Phoenix said. "I would appreciate that."

"All right, then. Let's consider that if you were to go forward with this initiative, what would be the good things, going in?"

"We have some really good people in our organization who, if they decided to support the work, could be assets to the initiative."

"That's good."

"I believe the initiative could allow for some breakthrough ideas to build the business."

"I like that one. What else?"

"Diversity is a reality at Xine-Ohp. I see it every day. It plays out in all sorts of ways, both to the benefit and detriment of Xine-Ohp. I have personally felt the effects of it in both ways. I think inclusion is a solution."

"I can see you're right about that. These are very weighty benefits. They're bound to outweigh most objections."

"They might, but I would need resources like money, people, time, buy in from the top leaders. I think it will be difficult to get those. Most of our top leaders are not fully knowledgeable on the subject. I fear a lack of clarity about results could cause the initiative to fail. I'm not sure Xine-Ohp's culture is ready for it."

"On the other hand," the VP of marketing and communications interjected, "our president is fairly enlightened on the subject. He has asked for this initiative. You would have his support. And as for the leaders not being knowledgeable, I don't agree with that. They may not have the full picture, but I think they may have some knowledge, and they would be receptive because of the president's interest. Wouldn't that be part of your job with the initiative—to enlighten people?"

Phoenix wasn't sure his mentor was accurate in his statements, but he couldn't argue with some of it. "Leveraging their support won't be easy. Leveraging inclusion won't be easy."

"*Easy* is what you're looking for, then?" the VP of sales asked. "I'm surprised at you, Phoenix."

Phoenix felt ashamed. He hadn't meant to sound lazy. "I just meant that resistance will come from all sides. I've already felt some of it when I was doing my interviews. There is no guarantee this will succeed."

"So you're looking for a guarantee as well?"

Phoenix ignored the chagrin he felt. "I say that because of previous attempts. This is an initiative like no other—"

"Will this be incorporated into your formal performance review?"

"I don't know. Nothing was said about it. I don't think so."

"As I see it, that could be good or bad depending on whether you succeed or fail." The VP of sales rubbed her thumb across her chin.

Phoenix swallowed. He didn't want to admit his biggest fear to his mentors—that if he went forward with the process, he would almost certainly lose his job, as his two predecessors had. That was the one negative he always came back to. He wanted to stay at Xine-Ohp, and his fear of losing his job overshadowed his pride in the Phoenix Principles.

He was tentatively ready to ask his mentors whether, overall, the good outweighed the bad. He wished someone could tell him definitively what to do. He was just about to open his mouth to ask the question when the VP of sales spoke again, seeming to have read Phoenix's mind. "Your decision to kill the diversity initiative may be a short-term solution. Certainly, it will get you off the hook. I honestly doubt whether you'd even get another assignment, but, if you did, it wouldn't be nearly as risky or challenging. The odds are that if you scrap this project, you'll guarantee the end of your career at Xine-Ohp. My opinion is that it wouldn't be your best move to say 'no' to the president."

"You need to think with a more can-do attitude," the VP of marketing and communications added.

"In other words, I really don't have a choice?"

"Of course you do," both mentors said simultaneously.

"I don't think you're seeing your choices with any precision. Think about it some more. I'm going to eat my lunch. I'm starving," said the VP of sales.

Phoenix picked up his fork and moved a tomato around the edge of his salad bowl. He had no appetite.

The VP of sales chewed her steak for a while and then said, "You're thinking that if you go forward, you will either succeed or fail, most likely fail, and if you reject the project, you'll save yourself the risk. But I'm telling you the opposite is true. Going forward, giving it everything you've got, will give you the best chance to succeed. Holding back will be certain death to your career at Xine-Ohp. But you could choose to work somewhere else. That's an option as well."

"That's a great choice," Phoenix said without enthusiasm.

But as Phoenix thought about their conversation, he realized that more than his job was on the line. His character was at stake as well. He didn't want to be known as a quitter. Mere weeks ago, he'd had a brilliant future or so he had thought. He wanted his good reputation back. His mentors were advising him that going forward, taking on the project, was the only way to do that. If only he could believe it. "If I lead this inclusion initiative, what can I do to give myself the best chance of succeeding?"

"There are no guarantees," the VP of sales warned. "After you've assembled your team of the Best People, let them help you create the Compelling Purpose. Then you'll be assured that it's work that others can buy into, modify, and own. That's the only way you'll get top leaders to buy into it. I know you don't think the support is there, but if you have the vision, people will follow."

The VP of marketing and communications thoughtfully added, "In addition, you must find others in the organization who can be advocates and champions for the work."

The VP of sales said, "You need to make sure all your team members are equally vested in and educated on the five success elements you've identified. That will clarify what your purpose is and how the work will be done."

"I think attaining a Solid Infrastructure for our work depends on its alignment with other important work, and we must always observe the norms of Xine-Ohp's culture," Phoenix said. "I need to make it perfectly clear to my team that these will be critical factors." Phoenix looked up to see both his mentors smiling at him.

"As a part of that, you'll have to partner with others to get the work done in the field. It won't really be owned by anyone if you do all the work yourself," the VP of marketing and communications added. "You must get other functions involved, like marketing, HR, research, sales, etc., but you should request to report directly to the president. It was his idea after all. And even if it weren't, it only makes sense for someone at or near the top of the organization to oversee it. His commitment will be an important factor."

"Most certainly," Phoenix agreed.

"That's good," the VP of sales commented.

The VP of marketing and communications continued. "Also, when you have outlined your Strategic and Measurable Actions, consider some hard measures as well as the softer ones—quantitative and qualitative—to track results and verify the ROI. Otherwise, the results will be merely anecdotal and may not be taken as seriously as they should be. Then put those results into well-formulated reports consistent with other reports we use."

"Be flexible and willing to continuously modify and adjust your approach. See what works and what doesn't and go from there," the VP of sales said.

"Communicate heavily. I can help you out there with more specific advice later on," added the VP of marketing and communications.

"When you have meetings, don't get stuck in the idea of having 100% consensus. Use the 80/20 rule. When 80% of your team agrees, go with it," recommended the VP of sales.

"Phoenix, you must be willing to take risks. You must believe the work you're doing is best for the company. Live it. Don't be afraid of it," the VP of marketing and communications advised.

Phoenix very nearly said he wasn't afraid but stopped as the words were forming. He couldn't deny it. He was afraid.

"Be willing to learn and grow along the way, share the success, look for nothing in return, and ultimately be willing to turn this process over to someone else at some point. That's what your renewal principle is all about," VP of sales said.

The more Phoenix thought about his mentors' advice, the more profound it seemed. These weren't just personal success factors. The points they'd made outlined some basic infrastructure requirements for leading a successful diversity/inclusion initiative at Xine-Ohp. They would also apply to leading any change initiative in any company.

Phoenix jotted some notes quickly on a napkin. He wanted to remember his mentors' advice and one day evaluate himself against them. He could use them as his personal benchmarks for success.

Then he looked at his watch. They had been sitting at their table for more than two hours. Phoenix felt a little guilty for keeping his mentors over their allotted time. "Thank you both," he said. "You've given me a lot to think about. I'm wondering—well, regardless of my decision—" Phoenix broke off in mid-sentence because he felt a little shy about asking to be reassured that they would still be there to guide him.

"Regardless of your decision, I'll still be here for you, Phoenix," the VP of marketing and communications told him.

"Absolutely," agreed the VP of sales. "As long as you keep your word to pay for my lunch." They all laughed, and Phoenix paid for the lunch personally, not even thinking of using his expense account.

As they walked to their cars, the VP of marketing and communications stopped him once again. "If you have a few more minutes, I'd like to tell you a story. It's a metaphor for putting your whole heart into anything you do. I've always found stories and metaphors helpful when I have important decisions to make."

Phoenix understood. "I like storytelling. My father used to tell me stories."

"Then you'll like this one. *A warship of an ancient civilization sailed to an island to do battle with an enemy who had plundered their own shores many times. When the ship approached the island, the warriors realized they were significantly outnumbered. In all probability, they would die in battle that day. Some of them wanted to go back, but the ship's captain obstinately ordered all hands ashore. The captain remained on the ship. As the disheartened warriors headed resolutely into battle, the captain set fire to the ship and then climbed into a smaller boat to row to shore. Flames from the ship shot up everywhere. The warriors thought the captain had gone mad. 'Are you crazy?' they shouted. 'You've eliminated our only chance of escape. You have assured our destruction.' The captain looked at them with an incredible intensity in his eyes and said, 'Fight hard. Today we sail home on our* enemy's *ship!' And so, realizing the commitment they had to make, they fought the battle of their lives and destroyed their enemies. Out of the fire and destruction of their own ship, the warriors were given new life.*"

The VP of marketing and communications said nothing more. He turned and walked away. Phoenix felt the impact of his mentor's lesson about opportunity and commitment.

He contemplated his mentor's words far into the night. He knew he had arrived at an important junction on the road to his future. Did he have the courage, like the ship's captain, to set fire to his own ship? Could he, like the mythical phoenix bird, rise once again from the ashes of his own discouragement? Once he had made his decision, it would be a new and different life. For better or worse, there would be no going back.

Phoenix's Tips for Success

- Assemble the best people
- Be clear about your purpose and goals
- Get buy in from the top leaders
- Get others to be advocates and champions
- Make sure the team is vested in each of the principles
- Integrate principles into important work processes, culture, and values
- Partner with others to work in field and get other functions involved
- Report directly to the president or other top executive
- Use quantitative and qualitative tests to track results and report in documents consistent with corporate culture
- Be flexible
- Communicate heavily
- Use 80/20 rule for consensus
- Take risks to achieve work that is good for the company
- Learn, grow, and share success; then turn it over to someone else

The phoenix, awakened to the danger, began to sing a song so melodious and sad that the birds began to cry a great rain. The hunters were blinded by the rain of tears and could not see where to aim their deadly arrows. The phoenix then flew away in a flash of light.

CHAPTER NINE

THE AWAKENING

The next day Phoenix worried over her decision. She mulled over the story about the captain who burned his own ship to motivate his warriors. Like Phoenix, the warriors hadn't chosen their situation but had been thrown into it by the island raiders and their own captain. Phoenix had been thrown into her situation by the SVP of operations.

Certainly there was no greater commitment than fighting for your life. The warriors had battled with their heads, hearts, and hands because the stakes were so high. Continued discouragement and half-hearted enthusiasm would have led them to certain death.

Phoenix's life wasn't at stake, only her career. But her career was her life in a way. One of her biggest concerns was that if she failed, she would be a high-profile failure. That would mean personal and public humiliation.

Phoenix also recognized another issue that she'd felt surfacing for some time. How would she deal with her own diversity issues? Possibly it was a major part of her apprehension. Like everyone, she had her own cultural and personal biases. How could she lead this initiative? How would she encourage others to accept an ideal that she wasn't 100% sure she could carry out on a personal level?

She often wasn't sure where cultural biases crossed over into personal style. Should she be required to change her own personal style to "fit in" at Xine-Ohp? Wasn't the point of inclusion to accept and use many styles to the organization's advantage? If many styles could be accepted, why couldn't Xine-Ohp accept hers?

On the other hand, she realized that she would have to make some compromises and adapt to the more formal corporate style in order to communicate more effectively.

She was becoming more certain that Xine-Ohp was ripe for an inclusion initiative. The real question was: Would they accept her vision of it? It would be up to Phoenix to use her leadership ability to convince them. She believed her SVP thought she couldn't succeed.

Phoenix thought about how high-performing, successful leaders operated. They believed in their own visions and persuaded others to follow those visions. Once, Phoenix had thought of herself as a natural-born leader. Where had that self-confidence gone?

Her doubts about the entire initiative had been mostly doubts about *how* she would put it in place. She realized her doubts about the "how" had made her doubt the "whether"—*whether* the president and the SVP would approve her plan, *whether* Xine-Ohp would accept her plan, *whether* her mentors would stand by her.

It ran contrary to her self-sufficient nature to feel so small and powerless, looking to everyone else to assure her success. Did it matter so much what others thought? Her mentors had helped her understand that her attitude was critical to success. They had also pointed out that if she didn't commit herself to this project, she was doomed at Xine-Ohp.

The events of the past few weeks illustrated to her that success was not determined by her situation. It was determined by what was inside her head. Courage wasn't necessarily about experiencing confidence or eliminating fear; it was a commitment, a decision to move forward with honor in spite of the fear.

Her ability to succeed rested on her own shoulders. Again, the message from her mentor's story rang loud and clear. To be fully committed, she must engage her heart and her hands as well as her head. Only then would she lead others to follow that vision.

Phoenix's thoughts turned to the process she'd discovered. Did she believe in the Phoenix Principles? Yes. They were sound. Her mentors had agreed on that. They had encouraged her.

In fact, by viewing the situation through a less doubt-driven lens, she could almost see inclusion happening at Xine-Ohp. She had developed the Phoenix Principles to implement the initiative. She might be a bit shaky in the confidence department, but she *would* commit to this project. She would give the Phoenix Principles the wings to fly.

She thought about the story her adoptive father had told her about the mythical bird for which she had been named. The myth spoke of the importance of being willing to change, being tested by fire, and succeeding in the face of insurmountable obstacles. This was her birthright—to arise from the ashes of her old self and be reborn into a newer and stronger creature. In fact, it was the birthright of every individual or human institution; each only had to lay claim to it.

The phoenix flew on, alone now, to the farthest palm tree on the edge of an uninhabited desert. At the top of the tree, it built a nest with the fragrant spices and incense that it had so carefully gathered and tucked among its brilliant feathers.

CHAPTER TEN

POINT OF NO RETURN

Phoenix moved forward. He knew this project was right for Xine-Ohp whether they were ready for it or not. Eagerness showed in his eyes and in his behavior. Phoenix had answered the challenge and had responded as all innate leaders do, with increased enthusiasm and energy.

First, he put together a presentation for the SVP that outlined his ideas and requirements. He needed to engage a diverse group of top performers and get them to commit to the process. They would be competent, committed team members. He would find people who would be as eager as he was to demonstrate their commitment.

Time was important to Phoenix and to Xine-Ohp as well. He couldn't afford to let the plans for the initiative linger. He needed to create a discovery process for his future team that would truncate the time needed for the Best People to make their decisions and take responsibility for the process. Individuals might need different data based on how they processed information. For some, like his mentor in sales, Phoenix knew statistics would be critical; for others, like his former boss, the VP of operations, it would be the plan and the process. There would be those, like the president, for whom the vision and mission would be the important factors. Still others, like his mentor in marketing and communications, would consider the impact on people to be the essential ingredient.

Phoenix was already beginning to see how inclusion affected his approach to the work. He would have to create ways to present the same plan with different emphases. One thing everyone would want to see was the return on investment.

With these things in mind, Phoenix placed the call to the SVP's executive assistant to schedule an appointment. He asked for two hours.

"I could give you something toward the middle of next month," the assistant offered.

"That's five weeks away," Phoenix objected.

"That's the best I can do unless you want a shorter time slot. She's been very busy lately."

"No," Phoenix said even though he was disappointed. "I'll take it." He had a ton of work to do in preparation for the meeting. Though he was fired up and ready to go, the extra time could work to his advantage.

And so, with a feeling of curbed excitement, but more determined than ever to create the best presentation of in his life, Phoenix spent many long days putting the presentation together. He had to turn the Phoenix Principles into a viable, working process.

If—*when* his proposal was approved, his team would bring it to life. His new team, he vowed, would not fall prey to the pitfalls of most diversity councils and diversity departments, which were often created in reaction to a crisis with no clear purpose or common set of outcomes. His team of the Best People would have the power to accomplish significant results rather than be merely well intentioned.

Phoenix envisioned a team of high achievers who represented a broad cross section of organizational levels and thinking processes—in fact, all aspects of diversity. His high-performing team would consist of diverse, self-motivated, strategic, talented, competent, and committed members who would always be eager to learn and grow.

Phoenix and the Best People would find a way to get budgeting and other resources. They would insist on quantitative and qualitative analysis rather than anecdotal results. They would incorporate clear expectations and measurable outcomes to assess effectiveness. They would report this information in well-crafted documents consistent with Xine-Ohp's culture and then transfer what they'd learned back to the organization. As his team's role evolved and the company's needs changed, they would provide highly effective documentation to reinforce the process.

Their measurable results would be tied to business objectives that would increase shareholder value, owner equity, and/or corporate goodwill. He would insist on a compelling purpose, a clear and well-crafted charter, and a definite scope of authority for his team. Xine-Ohp's leadership would take an active role in supporting the team's objectives. The entire process would be integrated into the company culture by aligning it with the company's goals and communicating across the organization through all the normal channels. Overall, Phoenix's vision was a lofty ideal, but one that would be worthy of Xine-Ohp.

Phoenix would have to fly solo for a while, though he would solicit some input from others along the way. To be effective, the plan would have to be "shaped up the ladder" in accordance with Xine-Ohp's culture. That meant getting buy-in from the top leaders in a progressive manner that would start with getting key stakeholder ownership.

Phoenix shaped his initial vision into a communication and sales document that addressed the ROI five-year growth plan via references to changing market forces and a competitive analysis that focused on the need for innovative product development. He referenced the need for risk management and cost containment associated with employee or customer suits. Additionally, he aligned documents with the organization's mission and vision. He included references to recruiting and keeping great talent. Last, he tied inclusion to Xine-Ohp's community-based initiatives.

Though Phoenix had an altogether daunting task before him, he felt very satisfied at the close of each day because his decision had been made. He was past the point of no return. His commitment was total.

In some ways, he was now a different person from the Phoenix who had started this project. It had made him more true to himself. His fire had been lit from within. He was preparing for the battle of a lifetime.

Some Keys to Linking Diversity
and Inclusion to Business Principles

- Compelling business opportunities
- Connection to the ROI five-year growth plan
- Changing market forces and innovation (internal and external)
- Competitive analysis
- Customer, community, shareholder, and employee impact
- Corporate values alignment
- Cost containment and risk management

The phoenix turned its face to the sun and anointed itself with light while the sun claimed it for its own. Soon the nest ignited, and the flames rose up to the very heavens. The phoenix wept tears of balsam as it claimed its birthright.

CHAPTER ELEVEN

THE ANOINTING

Phoenix prepared intensely for the meeting with the SVP of operations. She reviewed several past presentations that had been well received by the SVP. Then she reviewed her own information and organized it in a fashion consistent with the way these other successful projects had been presented. This was a new experience for Phoenix. She liked to think of herself as original and creative. In the past, she might have designed the presentation to fit her own criteria of excellence. This time she understood that to be effective, to give her presentation the best opportunity for success, she had to present in a style consistent with Xine-Ohp's culture.

Also, she referred to her notes from her initial meeting with the SVP. The SVP had mentioned operations efficiency, getting the best work out of the best people, and providing improved customer interfaces. Legal exposure had also been an issue. She wanted to be sure the SVP knew that her concerns had been considered and addressed.

Phoenix tried to predict what information the SVP would request. Who would the SVP consult for input? Through the office grapevine, she found out who the SVP's advisors were likely to be and how they were likely to process information.

Phoenix had arranged some in-depth discussions with people from various support functions, such as marketing, HR, research, sales, operations, and finance. As pleased as she was to gain access to their valuable information, she was more thrilled that she had identified some talented people as potential members for her team.

Once Phoenix assembled the initial information, she piloted her ideas with several groups, including her mentors and one of her

SVP's peers, the SVP of HR. Phoenix asked them to keep the information confidential. In her presentation, Phoenix explained each element of the process while advising them that it was a working draft to collect their input. It was a concept document that would ultimately be revised substantially by the SVP of operations, the Executive Leadership Team (which included the president), and later, if it was decided they could move forward in the process, her new team.

Phoenix was careful to relinquish any "pride in authorship." A few short weeks ago, her defensive attitude had made it difficult for her to listen well and receive feedback. She had learned since then that changes aren't a sign of weakness. Asking others to add their unique perspectives made the work stronger. Phoenix was proud of her project and looked forward to others' input on her ideas.

Phoenix did, however, clearly articulate her ownership of the final outcome and reserved the right, as the leader of the process, to make the final decision. She found that people were pleased to add their thoughts and appreciated being included. When she had to make a difficult decision, she relied on the 80/20 rule. If 80% of the reviewers wanted a change, she went with it. If not, she kept her original wording.

Phoenix felt she had developed a compelling business purpose, admittedly a high-level view of the plan. The team would ultimately develop the more practical aspects of the plan.

The first part was data driven. It included industry trends and demographic shifts; sales and account penetration by markets and demographics; operational efficiency reports based on functions; legal expenditures affecting the company; and key outcomes from external and internal initiatives, including the most likely objections to a diversity approach for solving business problems and enhancing opportunities.

The second part contained the sales strategy. It overviewed the proposed initial focus areas (based on the company's ROI five-year growth plan) to leverage inclusion and increase market share, increase operational efficiency, improve the corporate culture, and reduce risk and liability exposure. It proposed the structure, role, and scope of authority of the team. It outlined communication and education considerations, and corporate culture enablers and supporters of the initiative.

The third part outlined some general plans. These included a critical path schedule for start-up; a potential budgeting and resource allocation process; potential measurement, accountability, and reporting processes; and a list of potential functional partners and process owners.

In the fourth part, Phoenix summarized what material and personnel support might be needed. This included team members; internal demographic data on associates and trends; support from the Executive Leadership Team, the SVP of operations, and other stakeholders; and support from HR, marketing, finance, research, and other functions. She outlined her personal hopes and concerns, and the predicted impact on the organizational culture.

Phoenix prepared the most comprehensive document that she had ever developed, including information on the negative impact of diversity. Although Phoenix did not personally agree with that particular view, it was important for the SVP to get a 360-degree view of diversity and inclusion.

There was one thing Phoenix still lacked. She was troubled about a name for the team. She understood now that a proper name was very important in Xine-Ohp's culture. It had to be short, memorable, and descriptive. It needed to be linked to the business, and it should absolutely be aligned with the ROI five-year growth plan.

Phoenix remembered from an anthropology class she'd once taken that in many societies around the world, the naming process for individuals is often a sacred event. Choosing a name is important. The name speaks of who you are, who you aspire to become, where you come from, where you want to go, and, most important of all, what you stand for. Phoenix felt her own name had been given appropriately. Phoenix needed such a name to describe the purpose of her team.

She had been commissioned to research diversity initiatives but had found a better focus—inclusion. One thing Phoenix knew was that she would eliminate both the words "diversity" and "council" from the name.

"Diversity" already had a negative connotation because of its past association with legal mandates and affinity groups that often did not work well. Certainly she would need to educate the organization on the meanings and appropriateness of these concepts, but she wanted her initial focus to remain on inclusion.

The word "council" had a connotation of either a government agency or a group of people sitting around a table and pontificating on various ideas. Though this was not necessarily what a council did, the term was not consistent with the culture of Xine-Ohp. She had, in fact, never heard the word "council" used there, except when discussing diversity.

She couldn't keep calling her process the Phoenix Principles. She needed a real name that both embraced the principles and created energy in Xine-Ohp's culture.

She recalled of one of her early interviews with a line staff member who stated, "We don't need councils; we need partners in action." The statement resonated with her mentors' earlier comments about linking the initiative to the business.

"Partners." Phoenix said the word slowly. The term implied that the team would not own the initiative but collaborate with other functions, departments, and leaders. The name must be tied to the ROI and inclusion. Return on Investment Partners for Inclusion. That was rather lengthy. Return on *Investment* ... ROI. Return on *Inclusion* ... ROI. ROI Partners! Why not? It was memorable and descriptive. The "I" could stand for *investment* or *inclusion*. Short, memorable, and descriptive. Perfect. *ROI Partners*, she thought. The name had been around all along, just waiting for her to recognize it.

She almost wept as the fire of her enthusiasm drove her forward. Phoenix felt she had created an awesome plan from one part fear, one part enthusiasm for the Phoenix Principles, and one part her profound belief in the potential of inclusion to affect the revenues of the company. She was ready to meet with her boss.

≈

When the flames died down, there was no sign of the phoenix. Only a pile of red ashes remained inside the nest. As the ashes cooled, they began to move. A small, ugly worm emerged.

CHAPTER TWELVE

CHANGE IN PARADISE

Phoenix couldn't wait to present the program to his SVP. It was going to be the presentation of a lifetime, and he was ready to go. Since Phoenix's initial meeting with her to talk about the diversity initiative, they had seen each other occasionally in the course of their daily work. The subject of the diversity initiative, however, had not been mentioned. Phoenix had thought that, at the very least, the SVP should have asked how the research was going. Every time their paths had crossed, the SVP had been focused on other issues, so Phoenix had been reluctant to bring up the subject.

Phoenix again wondered whether the SVP cared about the project, but he also admitted he couldn't be sure whether his perception of her attitude was accurate. In any case, he appreciated the time she had given him to grow, learn, and discuss the project with others. The process had been quite different from any other assignment he'd ever had. It had required him to learn a lot, very quickly, about a subject with which he had been only vaguely familiar. All phases of the process—the information gathering, his own process of deep reflection and discovery, sharing with others, and even the emotional upheaval he'd gone through—had prepared him to discuss, present, and advocate for the ROI Partners.

By learning and sharing knowledge and receiving input from his mentors and others, he had learned to practice inclusion along the way. This collective, inclusive work had exceeded anything he could ever have achieved by himself. He could hardly believe that just a few weeks ago he was considering a plan to exit the project. How different things looked now!

Phoenix smiled as he remembered the SVP's earlier challenge to him. "You were looking for new challenges," she had said. "Let's see what you can do with this." It had indeed been a challenge rather than an insult.

His confidence in himself had grown. Phoenix admitted that when he felt confident, he sometimes had a tendency to be arrogant. He'd have to be careful about that. He arrived at the SVP's office a few minutes early for his 10:00 appointment. On his way across the lobby, he passed the SVP of HR, who was leaving. Phoenix spoke to him, and he answered with an absent-minded "good afternoon" before the elevator doors opened and he hurried inside. There was a lot of activity outside the SVP's office. Several regional VPs arrived and hurried in, one after the other, and then several other executives left the office just as quickly. Phoenix approached the executive assistant's desk.

"Oh, Phoenix, I'm sorry. I forgot to call you. Your meeting will have to be postponed until sometime later today." The woman looked at her watch and then consulted the computer screen. She smiled apologetically. "I can give you only one hour. Can you come back at 4:00?"

One hour? How could he give his presentation in an hour? His previous insecurities returned. He feared the inclusion process would not be valued. Had all his brilliant work been done for nothing? Was it going to be a waste of time after all? Would the SVP even bother to listen to his plan?

So much for arrogance, he thought. He'd been pumped to do the presentation. Now he felt totally deflated.

Phoenix tried not to show the SVP's assistant his frustration and disappointment. It wasn't the assistant's fault. "Okay," he said with a sigh of resignation.

Phoenix found it hard to concentrate on anything for the next several hours while waiting for the meeting. He attempted to contact his mentors, but neither was available. He pulled up his presentation on the computer and tried to shorten it, but every point seemed important and impossible to cut. Finally, he gave up and went to lunch with a colleague. In the early afternoon, he returned a few phone calls, but nothing he did completely diverted his mind from his presentation for the SVP. He checked his watch often.

Time crawled.

Just before 3:00, he received a call from the SVP's assistant. The meeting had been pushed back to 4:30, but he would still have "close to an hour."

Phoenix found it hard to control his anger, but he knew he must. It wouldn't do any good to be sullen. It was more important to cut the presentation. He opened the file and got to work.

While he worked, he was thinking of something one of his mentors had told him when they'd first met: "People will always find time for things they're interested in. They'll provide short time lines if they want to get out of something." The SVP, who had charged him with this project in the first place, was trying to get out of listening to his presentation. The realization did nothing for Phoenix's self-confidence.

Shortly before 4:30, Phoenix made the trip to the SVP's office and sat in the reception area for the second time that day. The executive assistant offered Phoenix a forced little smile that actually increased his anxiety. There was still a significant amount of activity, with people coming and going intermittently. When the door opened for the fifth time, the VP of sales exited the SVP's office. Phoenix greeted her. "I tried to call you earlier," he said, trying not to sound betrayed. After all, it wasn't his mentor's job to be available to him every moment.

"Oh?" she said absent mindedly. "I've been extremely busy. Back-to-back meetings all day. Listen, I'll give you a call later, eh?" She started to walk away and then stopped. "Oh! You had your big presentation this morning."

"Actually, no. It was pushed back to 4:30."

"Oh, yes. I'm sure it was." The VP of sales paused a moment and glanced back toward the SVP's door. She looked as if she intended to say something very serious and important. Instead, she cleared her throat. "I'm sure you'll do fine," she said.

Phoenix was disappointed in the platitude. He wasn't sure what he'd expected his mentor to say, but "you'll do fine" seemed luke-warm at best.

"Remember, challenges are a sign of engagement!" She gave Phoenix's forearm a light pat as the elevator dinged, and then she hurried off toward it.

Yeah, sure, Phoenix thought and sat down again to consult his watch, as he'd done every few minutes throughout the day. The administrative assistant finally called him at 4:35. Phoenix took a second to center himself before standing up. As he entered the office, he was surprised to see the VP of the eastern regional office sitting at the conference table in the corner. Phoenix wondered why the VP was there. This was *his* meeting with the SVP!

"Hello, Phoenix," the SVP said. "I apologize for the delay." The woman looked very tired. She was visibly stressed. "Because our time for your presentation has been shortened, I've asked our VP from the eastern region to attend. When you've finished your presentation, I have something to tell you."

Phoenix wondered what was going on and why the regional VP had to stay, but didn't have time to think about it much. The SVP ushered him immediately to the conference table. Fortunately, Phoenix had brought several handouts in case the SVP would want to distribute the information to the executive team or others. He handed a copy to each of them.

He opened his presentation by reviewing the assignment he'd been given and then asked whether the SVP or the regional VP had any opening questions before he began. The SVP indicated she had nothing to ask and then deferred to the VP. The regional VP abruptly stated, "I don't believe operations should be involved in diversity. I think this project is a waste of time and resources. I don't think we should have a diversity initiative. We don't have any diversity problems anyway."

Phoenix was surprised. He wasn't expecting an opening remark like this. Though he knew there would be resistance along the way— he'd encountered this attitude in his information gathering stage—he hadn't dreamed he'd encounter it this soon. He hid his concern and acknowledged the VP's opinion. Phoenix agreed with him that a traditional diversity initiative was not what was needed and wasn't the approach he would propose. He also agreed with him that the organization should not engage in anything that would be a waste of valuable resources, time, or focus. Phoenix disagreed politely, however, on the point regarding the role of operations and other functions in understanding diversity. "The real opportunity," he announced, "is in practicing inclusion. There are enormous opportunities to leverage inclusion in a way that will affect the business and support the company's ROI five-year growth plan."

Phoenix showed a slide of the Diversity Circle and explained that diversity is a fact of life and that its definition covers every current and future employee and customer of Xine-Ohp. Inclusion, he explained, is the process for leveraging diversity. Inclusion can affect everything that touches the business, including quality, cost reduction, and employee retention. When employees are valued and included, they become more committed and engaged in the work. An employee who cares about the work will do the work more efficiently. Employees who care about the business will take care of the business.

The VP listened politely and then said, "Tell me more about how inclusion can impact costs and the ROI five-year growth plan."

In response, Phoenix introduced his next topic: the concept of the ROI Partners as a vehicle to drive business results. He talked about the data as it related to Xine-Ohp. The VP listened carefully and asked some questions. Then he proceeded to question Phoenix's answers to his questions. No small point went unchallenged. His interest in every little detail of this part of the presentation taxed Phoenix's patience. He'd thought he would be presenting to the SVP with a general outline of the concepts of his plan. It was a good thing he'd been thorough in his information gathering and planning.

The SVP, however, seemed distracted from the beginning. Phoenix tried throughout the presentation to elicit a response from her, but she remained quiet, with only an occasional and sometimes ill-timed nod in Phoenix's direction. Phoenix had not previously appreciated the words of his mentor, "Challenges are a sign of engagement." He was beginning to understand them now. While the regional VP was "engaged" to the point of exasperation, the SVP's disinterest was more discouraging than the VP's rigorous questioning.

On a more positive note, early in their conversation, the VP stopped mentioning "diversity" and referred to the process as "inclusion." He was also very interested in the budgeting and resource allocation data. Phoenix explained, and the VP seemed to understand, that it was too early in the process to have all of the numbers fixed.

Although the VP seemed less interested in Phoenix's strategic plan of implementation, he listened carefully and asked a few questions. To illustrate the concept, Phoenix showed him a slide that looked like a wagon wheel with spokes sticking out from the hub. The spokes denoted the important strategic areas for implementation in a diversity or inclusion initiative.

Strategic Themes for Implementing Inclusion

The VP asked a few questions and offered some standard objections, which Phoenix addressed with expertise. The VP's favorite area was performance accountability measures. What would be measured? How would it tie into inclusion? How did Phoenix expect it to affect the company's bottom line? After Phoenix answered, the VP nodded thoughtfully, seemingly satisfied, and said he was surprised with the findings. Phoenix was pleased that his own recently deepened understanding of the business and the future of the company was impressive and compelling to this intensely engaged regional VP.

Phoenix finished the presentation by summarizing the basic concept of inclusion and the five elements of success (what Phoenix secretly called the Phoenix Principles) for the ROI Partners and reiterated how they could be tied to Xine-Ohp's ROI five-year growth plan. Though his exchange with the regional VP had been difficult, it was apparently successful. Phoenix was both annoyed and curious about why the SVP had not been more supportive.

By the time they finished, it was nearly 6:30. Phoenix was surprised at how fast the time had passed. The SVP acknowledged the time and apologized that they had gotten a late start and exceeded the allotted time. They thanked Phoenix for his presentation and asked him to leave the office for a few minutes while the two of them consulted.

Phoenix waited outside. His meeting had lasted almost two hours. They had made time for him after all. That was encouraging. As he paced the reception area, he remembered that before the meeting the SVP had mentioned that she had something to tell him. Phoenix wondered what it could be.

He walked to the restroom down a quiet hallway that was dark except for security lights. It was after 6:30 on Friday. Everyone had gone but the three of them. When Phoenix returned to the reception area, the regional VP was waiting for him. He held the door open, and Phoenix reentered the SVP's office. The SVP, however, was not there. "Sit down, Phoenix," the regional VP said. He reached into a briefcase and pulled out a file with Phoenix's name on it.

"Shouldn't we wait—?" Phoenix asked, looking around toward the door.

"No, that won't be necessary." The regional VP looked up at Phoenix for a second and then went back to perusing the file. After a moment he closed it and folded his hands on top of it. "Our meeting this afternoon has been a sort of performance review for you. I've been involved with diversity and mandated initiatives in the past and have not been impressed with the results. Even though I know it was the president's idea, I had every intention of recommending scrapping this diversity process and all those associated with it. As I said earlier, I think this diversity thing is a waste of time, money, and personnel. If you had said you were going to move forward with a traditional diversity approach, I would not have listened. I was fully prepared to offer you a severance plan. On the other hand, if you had recommended that the diversity initiative was a bad idea, I would have agreed with you. In both cases, I would have executed your discharge."

Phoenix was so shocked he couldn't choke out one word of reply.

"But you've proposed a bold new idea. I like your logic. This idea about setting up a team of ROI Partners to focus on increased profits for Xine-Ohp got my attention.

"As of today, I'm the new SVP of operations. My predecessor has decided to leave the company. An official announcement will be made on Monday. Right now, I'm in the process of picking my new team members. I like your methods, Phoenix. I'll plan to use them with my team. Oh, and yes, you *are* on my team if you want to be here. Your responsibility will be to make all that stuff on paper come to life. I think you'll realize when you put your plan into practice, there will be lots of problems you'll have to fix. I'll hold you accountable for the results. If you achieve them, you can hold me accountable to recommend you for a promotion in two years. I'll support you with the president and the Pipeline Committee. You have until noon on Monday to give me a final answer. I expect you to keep this process confidential until such time as we begin to implement it."

The new SVP of operations went on with his monologue while Phoenix sat in stunned silence. "I am a big advocate for growing our business, and you'll need to help me fully understand how inclusion will help. I believe the 'best people,' as you call them, are our most valued resources. I want only the best people on my team. I want people who are bold, innovative, adaptive, and confident— those who think about growth as exponential, not incremental. I expect you to pick your own team members wisely.

"I'll be available, as needed, on critical issues. I understand you've been relieved of all your other duties to focus 100% of your attention on this opportunity. I'd like to keep it that way. I'm going to give you some administrative support, but it will be minimal in the beginning. We'll meet together monthly for two hours or under emergency conditions if one should arise. You have the power to make this happen. I do not micromanage. I will challenge, push back, and shoot straight. I expect the same from you. Trust, good intentions, commitment, and integrity are important values for me. They are nonnegotiable characteristics of my team members.

"You and I will present a top-of-the-line plan to the president and Executive Leadership Team in thirty days. I'll have my assistant call you with the exact date and time. I'll expect you to have the ROI Partners ready to go in six months after our meeting with the president.

"Because we are between budget cycles right now, I expect you to have a full budget plan ready for the next budget cycle. I don't need to tell you that you will be fiscally accountable. Our shareholders' monetary interests must be protected. At the same time, we need to see some immediate ROI for the process and some projected plans for the long term.

"We'll run a prototype in operations to test the viability of a full-scale company initiative. I'm a big quality proponent, and you've shown me that quality has a potential link to inclusion. We'll start with that. We'll publish an annual report of our progress and our return on investment. Then we'll be prepared for the entire company to review, discuss, share, and debate its merits." The new SVP ended his barrage almost as quickly as he'd started. "Do you have any comments to make at this time?"

"Uh. No, sir. I agree with everything you've said." Phoenix could only blink and hope he remembered everything his new SVP had said. Though gruff, the man was detailed. He'd given Phoenix some precise expectations to live up to.

"Do you have any questions?"

Phoenix had never been more amazed in his life. He could only squeak out a few words, "No questions right now. Thank you." He was simultaneously frightened, happy, and confused.

He rose from the table and made his way to the door. The SVP walked him out and smiled for the first time all afternoon. "By the way," he said, "you've made great choices in mentors. The VP of sales was my mentor for many years. Now we're lifelong friends. I wouldn't be where I am today without her."

Without waiting for questions or replies, he closed the door, and Phoenix headed toward the elevators. On his way to the parking lot, he felt a bit saddened about the departure of the former SVP. Her sudden exit seemed ominous to Phoenix.

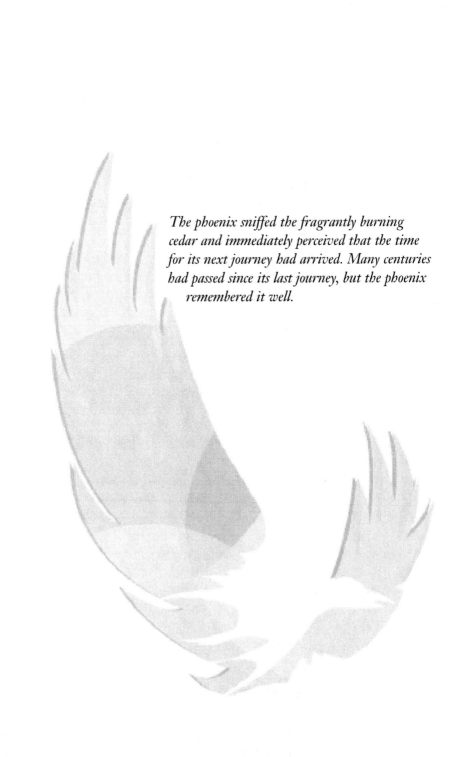

The phoenix sniffed the fragrantly burning cedar and immediately perceived that the time for its next journey had arrived. Many centuries had passed since its last journey, but the phoenix remembered it well.

CHAPTER THIRTEEN

NEW BEGINNINGS

Phoenix had never been so glad to see a weekend. What a week it had been. The new SVP had approved the continuation of the project after he'd almost decided to terminate her. Instead of a severance package, Phoenix had received the assignment to develop the ROI Partners. Her ideas had worked!

It was a beautiful weekend, and Phoenix sat on her balcony and made notes on everything the SVP had outlined. She also reflected on some other lessons she'd learned from the meeting. She'd been prepared, and that was invaluable. But her decision to be fully committed to the project had been the critical link to her success.

The situation had changed very quickly, so it had been necessary for Phoenix to be flexible. And the executives had been flexible with her. It was true that people make time for what's important to them.

The new SVP had set some specific time lines for the deliverables he expected, which gave the project some definition. This felt much more comfortable to Phoenix than being directed to "see what you can do with it and get back to me in a few weeks." And he'd promised Phoenix a budget. That was true commitment.

While Phoenix had presented the information geared toward the previous SVP, she had also included formats for people with various learning preferences so that anyone might be able to grasp the concepts immediately. Certainly her new SVP was an analytical thinker. He had latched onto the numbers quickly and asked endless questions about the systems and measurements.

Most importantly, if Phoenix hadn't linked inclusion to the business priorities of the company, she would have been scouting for an employment search firm on Monday. It would be imperative to the process to measure the progress and report the results.

Wasn't it ironic that the new SVP had been mentored by one of Phoenix's own mentors? Phoenix stopped in mid-thought. Her mentors had told her they would support and guide her no matter what. Phoenix was feeling rather humble now, realizing how much support she must have been receiving behind the scenes.

Things were not always as they appeared. Phoenix's thoughts returned to the previous SVP. Phoenix had assumed her lack of engagement meant she didn't care about the project. Phoenix had perceived that lack of interest as a personal insult. It was obvious now that the woman had more pressing personal priorities, which had nothing to do with Phoenix.

Phoenix also thought about the different reasons each had for engaging in the inclusion initiative. The president had his concerns about diversity issues, which had been vaguely communicated by the former SVP. With the research Phoenix had done, she interpreted those concerns as the need to improve productivity, reach multicultural markets, and manage risk. As for the previous SVP's motivation, she had been following the president's orders.

The new SVP, however, clearly saw inclusion as a tool to accomplish revolutionary business objectives. People often saw inclusion as the "right thing to do." While the social aspect was very strong, Phoenix felt more comfortable having the leadership at Xine-Ohp support inclusion as a business initiative. Actually, Phoenix herself had embarked upon the journey because it was a career requirement, but it had grown to be more. She'd increased her understanding of the business rationale and the social incentives for inclusion. The SVP had empowered Phoenix to achieve results by placing his trust and confidence in her. She believed she was becoming a better leader and a more evolved person as a result of her journey—and the voyage was just beginning.

The SVP also recognized that Phoenix would need time to put together the team of ROI Partners. Six months seemed like a reasonable length of time to accomplish this task. Phoenix had already spent substantial time understanding inclusion and the Phoenix Principles. This advance work would expedite and truncate the learning process, but there would be the time-consuming process of transitioning the individual members into a team.

Once the team was in place, the ROI Partners would have to produce substantial business results rapidly to prove their value to the business. Using a pilot program to perfect the process before applying it company wide was a fair proposition and was consistent with many of the company's ventures.

Phoenix noted that the SVP had grasped the idea that quality and inclusion were linked. Quality was a major corporate initiative tied to the ROI five-year growth plan.

As Phoenix looked over her notes, the sheer size and depth of the project engulfed her. As reality set in, she again felt a bit over-whelmed about her assignment. She remembered the words of the former SVP, "This is a corporate-wide initiative with great expo-sure and interest from the top." These words both elated and frightened Phoenix. Getting the ROI Partners up and running quickly was essential. Step one of the Phoenix Principles, getting the Best People, would be an exciting challenge.

Phoenix had thirty days to prepare to co-present with her new SVP to the president and Executive Leadership Team. Four critical tasks must be completed during that time. She jotted them into a short e-mail to her mentors to get their feedback.

The first one was to revise her presentation. She gave herself two weeks to make the changes based on some of the questions and input from the new SVP. Then she would forward this revised information to him to see whether he had any further recommen-dations.

Second, she would start pulling together the Best People. She would solicit help from human resources to help with this task and to create an orientation process for the ROI Partners. She would also seek their support and guidance for the transformation of her people into a high-performing team within six months.

Third, she would put together a position description to clarify her new role, scope of authority, and the SVP's expectations. She wanted to make sure both she and the SVP understood each other precisely. Later, she could use the position description to write a performance review to document delivery of those expectations. Phoenix was taking the SVP at his word that she could be promot-ed in two years.

Fourth, she would develop a critical path schedule for important time lines, tasks, budgets, deliverables, and deadlines, as well as a reporting process for progress similar to the format Xine-Ohp used for other initiatives.

It was a weekend of hard thinking. On Sunday afternoon, Phoenix made two calls to tell her mentors about the meeting and arranged an early lunch with both of them the next day.

During their lunch, her mentors shared some important information about the new SVP that would be helpful to her and provided input on the performance review process document Phoenix had created. Her mentors affirmed that her plan and focus were on target.

Phoenix was curious about the former SVP and wanted to ask them about her but felt questions might be inappropriate. At one point in the conversation, however, Phoenix's mentors suggested that Phoenix send the former SVP a letter. "Whether on purpose or by chance, she has provided you with an opportunity of a lifetime. It would be good to acknowledge that favor. You never know."

The SVP of Marketing asked, "What was the new SVP's reaction when you called to let him know you've accepted his offer to be on his team?"

Phoenix was startled by the question. She realized that in her excitement, she'd forgotten to make the call. She looked at her watch. It was after 11:30! He'd given her until noon for her final answer. Her mentors laughed as she grabbed her cell phone and hurriedly punched the numbers. The SVP didn't answer, so Phoenix left a message on his voice mail. Then she excused herself, paid the check for her mentors' lunches, and rushed back to her car to type a quick text message to the SVP's e-mail to reinforce the phone call. At two minutes before noon, Phoenix received a short reply from the new SVP. "Welcome aboard. I'm pleased you're on my team. I expect great things from you."

At one minute before noon, Phoenix sent her reply, "You won't be disappointed. Thank you!"

Phoenix smiled and then returned to the office to write the note to her former SVP. It was a small thing to do, but Phoenix felt it was important.

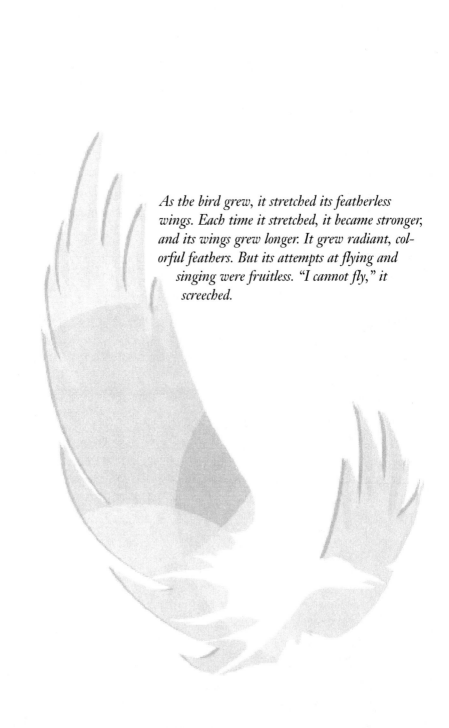

As the bird grew, it stretched its featherless wings. Each time it stretched, it became stronger, and its wings grew longer. It grew radiant, colorful feathers. But its attempts at flying and singing were fruitless. "I cannot fly," it screeched.

CHAPTER FOURTEEN

THE CRUCIBLE

For the next thirty days, Phoenix worked diligently preparing for the upcoming meeting with the president and the Executive Leadership Team. He read every report on the company since its founding in 1902—or at least he felt like he had. Using some of his findings and the suggestions his new SVP had made, he worked to improve his presentation. He wanted it to be flawless when he delivered it. Then he met with the key stakeholders, mentors, and members of every department and function in the company—in short, everyone who could give him feedback. In fact, he was starting to think he might be wearing out his welcome in several places.

It was a consuming, but energizing, task.

The meeting was to be held in the boardroom on the twenty-fifth floor. Phoenix arrived early to set up his equipment. He'd been to the twenty-fifth floor before, and it had a totally different atmosphere from any other. All the senior executives, except the SVP of operations, had their offices there. It was intimidating. The rich-colored, plush carpet matched the decor of the reception area on the first floor. The rest of the building used short-nap commercial carpet in a neutral blue-gray. An expensive interior designer had obviously carefully arranged the pictures, original paintings, limited-edition prints, and other *objets d'art*. The mahogany furniture gleamed with a soft, rich patina. It was rumored that even the air was different here, imported from Valhalla, the mythological Hall of the Gods.

Phoenix was nervous but excited. It almost seemed as if something magic were about to happen. If the meeting went well,

Phoenix envisioned laurel wreaths adorning his office cubicle when he returned. Of course, if the meeting didn't go well, he would likely be looking through the garbage can for the severance package that had been so generously offered to him a month ago by his SVP. But Phoenix had decided not to think negative thoughts. He was determined to believe in the best possible outcome.

The buzz had been hot on the company grapevine that Phoenix had a meeting with the president. Everyone had been curious. Of course, they knew Phoenix was working on an inclusion initiative, but Phoenix had known better than to discuss the details. He had, however, tapped the grapevine to find out whether the SVP of operations had discussed the ROI Partner approach with other senior executives. His reconnaissance had been sparse, with no clear indication of the thoughts or attitudes of the Executive Leadership Team toward the initiative. The lack of information wasn't surprising considering the initiative was supposed to remain a confidential matter until its approval and rollout.

Phoenix had also gathered as much information as he could about the "pecking order," the decision-making process, and the individual thinking styles of the members of the Executive Leadership Team, a.k.a. the "Infinite Nine," as they were called by some for the seemingly infinite power they held in the company.

The president was obviously the leader and primarily a strategic thinker focused on the future of Xine-Ohp and its position in the industry. The two other major players were the controller/chief operating officer, an analytical thinker who liked data and numbers, and the chief legal officer, who, like the SVP of operations, was a planner by nature and training. Because operations was the largest department in the company, the former SVP of operations had been a member with substantial influence. Because the new SVP had been on the team for only a month, it was hard to say whether he would have the same influence. Still, Phoenix was glad the new SVP would be there to co-present with him and support him even if the SVP was the newest team member. Phoenix couldn't imagine doing the presentation without him. The remaining five members were approximately equal in influence on the Executive Leadership Team and were a mixed bag of another strategist, two other analytical thinkers, and two who were primarily focused on people issues.

Overall, they were a well-balanced group in terms of their thinking styles. Their collective decision-making process would be heavy on data analysis and strategy, balanced by the planning and people-oriented perspectives.

In Phoenix's opinion, this meeting would be the "moment of truth" or "crucible" for Xine-Ohp on inclusion. He'd learned that few companies ever had that kind of "defining moment" about diversity or inclusion in which they understood the need for active involvement. Companies "did" diversity because it was considered a "nice thing to do." In some cases, company leaders merely tolerated the efforts of a few well-intentioned people. Many companies allocated a few dollars here and there in lieu of a real commitment. Those scenarios didn't require anyone to draw a line in the sand and say, definitively, "Yes, we will" or "No, we won't" or even "Yes, we will, but let's modify it." More companies needed to be committed and actively involved in diversity and inclusion, instead of avoiding the issues or merely tolerating attempts at solutions. Today, he and his SVP would be the catalysts for Xine-Ohp's "moment of truth."

If the Executive Leadership Team decided not to go forward with the plan, Phoenix would make sure they understood the price. He had graphs to prove they were currently losing money, talent, and efficiency from high employee turnover rates, some of which could be attributed to intolerant behavior. He had figures on the basic costs to start the initiative and the higher costs if they didn't. The prolonged dysfunction of isolated silos and the repressive nature of the top-heavy corporate culture far outweighed the temporary inefficiencies of starting the initiative. According to anecdotal evidence, the workforce was diverse, but the evidence needed to be benchmarked and measured. Soon Xine-Ohp would take possession of another company. Imminent havoc was possible as a result of mixing the corporate cultures. Phoenix knew that the positive results of the ROI Partners' work would far exceed the costs and adjustments.

Phoenix felt passionate about getting Xine-Ohp started along its inclusion journey. But sometimes companies or their leaders weren't ready. As disappointing as it would be if the Executive Leadership Team decided Xine-Ohp wasn't ready, he had to control his emotions.

If he didn't remain calm, he wouldn't be productive in his presentation. The factual and logical delivery of his vision and his data required an unruffled demeanor. His arguments had to be compelling and thoughtful, as well as passionate.

He also reminded himself that, as supportive as his SVP had been in offering him a place on his team, it wasn't over until it was over. If the Executive Leadership Team rejected his plan, might he still lose his job? Would the SVP find another good assignment for him, or would he say that he regretted the situation, but ... sorry?

Phoenix put that out of his mind for the moment. He was as prepared as he was ever going to be. He was ready to go.

When he had completed his setup, he waited in one of the supple leather chairs in the massive boardroom and looked out at the view from the twenty-fifth floor. He took a sip of the bottled water provided on the ornate credenza. He wondered what it would be like to be this far up in the company and looking out at the world from a powerful position as a senior executive or board member.

One of the double doors opened, and Phoenix's SVP of operations entered. He walked over to Phoenix and shook his hand. Then, without preamble he said, "I'm sorry, but there's been a change in plans. I won't be co-presenting with you after all, but I'll introduce you."

What was he saying? They had sixty minutes to present, which was an eternity on the twenty-fifth floor. Phoenix and his SVP had agreed on their roles for the presentation. Now Phoenix would be presenting *alone*? His stomach dropped. He'd been counting on the SVP. How could he back out at the last minute?

They heard voices in the hallway. The others were arriving. "Another thing, quickly," the SVP whispered. "I'm going on vacation with my family. We had planned to fly out tomorrow but had to change our flight plans. I'll have to leave as soon as the presentation is over in order to catch my flight in time."

"Will we have time for a brief discussion?" Phoenix asked.

"I'm afraid not. I'll be running as it is. My wife and family will be waiting for me out front."

Phoenix was crushed. The one person he depended on to support him had bailed out on the most important presentation of his career. He had dumped it all in Phoenix's lap. He couldn't even debrief because of his vacation plans.

In that instant, the presentation became another personal moment of truth for Phoenix.

As the others entered the room, their voices fell into hushed whispers. It felt to Phoenix as if the room temperature had dropped ten degrees. Never had he seen a more unyielding row of silent faces. Nine similar pairs of eyes stared at him.

The ways in which Phoenix was not like the others in the room had never been more apparent than they were right now. He swallowed hard and fixed a pleasant expression onto his face. He tried to appear confident and not show that he was intimidated. But while he studied them and gathered his wits, he felt the intensity in the room, and it was like none he'd ever experienced with any other group. Their faces were cold and unexpressive, but they had fire in their eyes.

The reality of the situation hit him full force. He was sitting at a table with the nine most powerful people in his company. Though he was scared, their genuine commitment to the best interests of Xine-Ohp and its shareholders, customers, and employees didn't escape Phoenix.

Phoenix sat near the front of what seemed to be the largest table in the world for nine people and waited for his introduction. The SVP of operations stood beside him at the head of the table. At least, Phoenix thought, the SVP would support the work in his opening remarks.

"I'd like to introduce you to Phoenix. He's going to propose a major corporate initiative of leveraging inclusion at Xine-Ohp. He has prepared the process and is asking for some of the company's best people to be assigned." Then the SVP stepped aside and took his own seat, down a few chairs from Phoenix.

Phoenix was stunned at the brevity of his introduction. It took all the willpower he had to keep the smile pasted on his face. His imagination went wild. It was a setup. The SVP was not committed to this project. He's out to get me. He doesn't care at all. But Phoenix couldn't dwell on the betrayal right now. He would have to be a good actor and pretend it didn't bother him.

He took a deep breath and stood. "Thank you," he said, smiling warmly and nodding toward the SVP of operations. As he began, his heart beat hard against his ribs, and the image came into his mind of a ship's captain—far from home, fighting his enemies, setting fire to his own ship. Phoenix was about give the most important performance of his career. He would sink or swim. *Alone.*

But with total commitment.

Phoenix knew that to hesitate now would be to lose them, so he dove immediately into his introduction, a two-minute "elevator speech," as many people called these types of brief overviews. By using it many times over the past couple of months, he had refined it so that it was compelling and thought provoking. "Our ROI five-year growth plan is the key to the success of our company. With today's diverse consumers driving the economy, it will be impossible to reach our financial objectives without leveraging the principles of inclusion." Phoenix paused, looking briefly at each person around the table. Doubt was on most of the faces; others looked smug and others curious. But, whatever their opinions, they were definitely listening.

"Our shareholders, customers, and employees depend on us to develop and deliver the breakthrough products, services, and solutions they deserve. Our competitors are in active pursuit of our business and are competing for our best talent. As an internationally recognized company, we must do our best to grow and become a market leader—or fall behind. You know all this, of course." He smiled warmly at them and paused to let his statement sink in before plunging into his bold vision of the ROI Partners.

"I'm proposing the formation of a diverse team of the Best People to help achieve our goals. They'll be guided by a Compelling Purpose, validated by Strategic and Measurable Actions, strengthened by a Solid Infrastructure, and invigorated by a plan for Structured Renewal. Without this plan for inclusion, even if we achieve our goals, we won't sustain our success for long." He knew his last comment was an aggressive statement. He believed it to be true. As he scanned the faces around the table again, he saw a few eyebrows raised in surprise.

"I call this team of the best, brightest, most diverse and talented people in our organization the ROI Partners. They'll help Xine-Ohp reap millions of dollars from financial, operational, and cultural enhancements to our business.

"This innovative work will be aligned with our standard business practices. While it will require a change in Xine-Ohp's company culture, that is, in the *way* things get done, it is consistent with Xine-Ohp's values and with its tradition of quality, excellence, and innovation. I've come here today to seek your active input, to invite debate, and ultimately to gain your support for this project." There were a few murmurs, but no one objected to anything he said. They weren't kicking him out, at least.

"If there are no questions, I'll start my presentation. I'm excited about sharing this data with you. I've also prepared preliminary strategies, plans, and protocols for your consideration. They're to be considered a working draft that may be refined by the Executive Leadership Team and, later, by the ROI Partners."

Phoenix's presentation was similar to the one he'd previously given to his SVP, which seemed like centuries ago. Certainly that first presentation had been great practice. He spent more time on the strategic considerations to accommodate the thinking style of the president. But he spent most of his time in the data and planning areas to address the thinking styles of the majority of the team. And, as expected, most of the questions occurred in this area. Phoenix truly appreciated the SVP of operations for helping him improve the presentation.

There were a few high points during the presentation when he felt the members of the Executive Leadership Team were on board with him. But there were many low points. The tone of some of their questions made Phoenix wonder why he was even making this presentation. He often longed for his SVP to speak up and show support, but he didn't. Phoenix felt totally abandoned, alone on the island and fighting for his life.

The questions kept coming at him. His advance intelligence had been correct. It was obvious to Phoenix that, aside from the president, the controller/COO and the chief legal counsel were the most influential. Throughout the presentation, eight members of the Executive Leadership Team fired at him from every direction and made him feel personally attacked by some of their comments. Whatever the question or concern, Phoenix always went back to the ROI five-year growth plan as the guiding document for his work. It was the sacred document, already conceived and blessed by this very group, the "Infinite Nine."

As one hour stretched into ninety minutes, Phoenix felt exhausted. It was the most grueling session he'd ever led. He drew on almost every experience he'd ever had to keep the session on a positive track. His every skill was tested, every competence weighed by these men with their tough questions, their contemplative frowns, and their crossed arms.

When there were no more questions, Phoenix closed the presentation, and the president thanked him. "You'll hear from us via the SVP of operations in a week or two." There were a couple of nods around the table. The president dismissed the group, and the SVP of operations quickly slipped out the door. The rest of the Executive Leadership Team left unhurriedly, murmuring among themselves without a word to Phoenix.

Phoenix packed his laptop as he fumed about the SVP's desertion. Judging by the executives' cold reactions to him, he had failed to convince them. Maybe he hadn't approached it the right way. Maybe he wasn't such a good actor, and his doubts and nervousness showed through. Perhaps he didn't have the right answers, or the data had been skewed. He hadn't expected to feel so very low. It was almost a *déjà vu* of the way he felt when he'd first been handed the assignment by the former SVP.

But surely he couldn't have been so far off base. He'd given them some useful information; he was sure of it. It would be agony to wait a week or more to learn their response. The SVP was on vacation for the next week, so there would be no input or debrief from him. They were smart people, he thought, if a bit cold. Why couldn't they just accept his project or reject it today? Why did he have to wait so long?

The worst part was feeling so alone. There was nobody to talk to for feedback. He decided he could at least call his mentors. They would know about the process and about dealing with the Executive Leadership Team. He sent an e-mail to the VP of sales and received an automated message in response. To Phoenix's consternation, she was on vacation, too. He called the VP of marketing and communications. He was out of town for a conference for the rest of the week. Phoenix was definitely feeling sorry for himself again, the one competency he would not want the Executive Leadership Team to see. But this was an excruciating situation, and he needed his mentors now more than ever. How would he survive the next week or two?

He slept fitfully that night as he gnashed his teeth and dreamed alternately of voids of darkness and pits of fire.

*And then, one day, the phoenix saw another
creature far below the palm tree. "I am lost," the
creature said. "Can you help me find my way?"
The phoenix looked out over the horizon and told
the creature what it saw and how to proceed.
"Thank you, my friend," the creature said.
With that, the phoenix felt its strength
return. It spread its wings and sang its
beautiful song with its sweet harmony of
five notes. It had grown to its former
majesty and was ready
to return to the forest.*

CHAPTER FIFTEEN

PURGATORY

There were no laurel wreaths on Phoenix's desk when she returned.
In fact, no one even asked her about the presentation. It was almost
as if she had become invisible, Phoenix thought. The silence was
intense.

Her coworkers had known about her meeting with the
Executive Leadership Team though she had kept the details confidential. She wondered if they were deliberately avoiding talking
about it in front of her. Were they jealous? Or did they think she
had failed and wanted to stay as far away from the subject as possible? Phoenix felt abandoned by her peers as well as her mentors
and the SVP of operations, who were all supposedly supporting
her. She was lonely and angry.

Because her SVP had relieved her of her other duties to work
on the inclusion project, she didn't have much to do to keep her
mind off her troubles. She tried to think about the process for
selecting the Best People, but could give it only a token effort.
What would be the use of working on it anyway? If they killed the
project, it would be wasted effort.

Consumed by the insecurity of not knowing the decision of the
"Infinite Nine"—and she thought of them with all the sarcasm the
term held—Phoenix made a few inquiries to her usual sources on the
office grapevine. Her attempts were met with silence. Nobody knew
anything, which was quite unusual because the corporate grapevine
at Xine-Ohp was often the most timely and reliable source of information in the company. In this case, however, there was not a single
word. Phoenix couldn't believe there was no information out there

anywhere. She was probably right about people thinking she was a failure. She had become a pariah.

Left in the dark, Phoenix's speculations only worsened. Her list of fears went on and on. Maybe something had happened to change her SVP's mind, and he didn't want to admit it. Perhaps as the *new-timer* on the "Infinite Nine," her SVP had no voice or influence. Maybe he'd never been in favor of this project, and it was all an elaborate setup. Possibly the "Infinite Nine" had someone else in mind to lead the project and would give that person all of Phoenix's hard work. Perhaps the "Infinite Nine" were all racists, ageists, sexists, elitists, idiots, or just plain mean. Maybe Phoenix hadn't done a good job. This one made her feel really bad, though underneath she couldn't really believe it was true.

Maybe the company was going out of business. No, that wasn't true either. She'd done enough research to know better than that. She was getting paranoid; that was the problem. She, too, probably should have taken a vacation this week. Everyone else was gone. She felt like her mind was on vacation. Although her physical body was showing up for work, her energy, spirit, and best thinking did not accompany her. They were wandering aimlessly in the land of doubt.

However, two interesting things happened to Phoenix during the week. Both involved people who were very different from the rest of the employees at Xine-Ohp. She had lunch with a person of an ethnic culture that was not represented by the dominant culture at Xine-Ohp. This person spoke of the impact of culture on products. Even colors were sometimes subject to cultural preferences or symbolism. They also discussed how negotiations in that person's culture were generally conducted. This encounter demonstrated to Phoenix how little knowledge she had about this person's culture, particularly its purchasing styles and preferences. Phoenix wondered how much Xine-Ohp could increase sales if they were more aware of the local culture where some of its products were sold.

The other encounter involved two people from two different functions who had been thrown together on a project and needed to work together more effectively. It wasn't that they didn't get along, but the subculture and protocols of their separate departments were so ingrained that it was difficult for them to get anything done.

Phoenix thought there should be some way to bridge the gap between them.

Phoenix dubbed these incidents her "inclusion learning moments." In fact, Phoenix was becoming aware that she thought about many things differently as she learned more about the implications of inclusion. She interpreted her learning moments as proof that inclusion was important and that it had an impact on the business. She feared she might not get the chance to prove it.

When Phoenix finally received a call from the SVP's executive assistant to schedule an appointment, she had mixed reactions. She was still angry and wanted to tell her SVP how she felt. But she was also anxious and curious to hear the decision of the "Infinite Nine." She prepared herself for a big letdown.

Phoenix arrived at the meeting early and was met by the executive assistant, who was much friendlier than she had been in the past. Phoenix had heard just that morning through the grapevine that the woman was much happier with her new boss and that she worked much harder for him. The rumors must be true, Phoenix thought, as the assistant ushered her into the SVP's office with a bright smile. The executive assistant had been with Xine-Ohp for eighteen years and had undoubtedly seen many people come and go. You lose some, and you win some.

Phoenix was surprised to find the SVP and the president in the office, both looking very pleasant. The president began, "I'm only going to stay a few minutes to share the decision of the Executive Leadership Team regarding your proposal. Afterward, you and your SVP will discuss next steps and other implications."

Other implications? That can't be good.

The president continued, "Overall we were impressed with your presentation. The information you shared was worth considering. It is different, to say the least, from what I expected when I threw out my idea to get a diversity initiative going. Honestly, the Executive Leadership Team has mixed opinions on the economic impact and viability of inclusion as an important business strategy. Our resources are tight, and you're requesting that we rethink some of our strategic thrust. This is difficult for us.

"Additionally, our individual and collective experiences on diversity, and what you call inclusion, have been somewhat limited.

Some of the team members think it's a fad, some feel it's not really an issue, while others think it may have some merit or is 'nice to do.' Because of this lack of total consensus, it would be easy for us to dismiss this proposal.

"However, you have presented us with a compelling business challenge. Perhaps an opportunity, eh? We're not convinced it has multimillion-dollar potential, but most of us do think it may have some significant growth potential. As I said, everybody on the team doesn't agree. In fact, some are outright against investing one dime in it. However, your SVP is a big supporter of this process—and of you."

Phoenix turned to the SVP in surprise. She certainly had not felt supported.

"We have decided to trust his judgment. To your credit, all the Executive Leadership Team members agreed on one thing. They were impressed by you, your depth of knowledge and understanding of our business, and the data you've collected. Even though all of them didn't agree with your proposal, several said they'd like to have you in their departments on a more meaningful assignment." The president smiled and then laughed aloud. "This is truly a compliment, Phoenix. We very seldom agree unanimously on anything.

"We've agreed to support the inclusion effort. We can't give you all the funding you asked for, but we will give enough support to say we're serious about our commitment. It will be enough for you to prove its value and contribution to the company's ROI. We expect you'll narrow the focus down and make sure we're working on the most important things. We expect you to measure your results. If the results are positive, more resources will follow. To start with, we'll support you in getting the Best People on the assignment.

"I'm designating your SVP to serve as my sponsor for the ROI Partners, and he has my official proxy. If you need my personal involvement for any critical matters, you and the SVP will have access to me. I will expect a revised, comprehensive, and focused plan, along with a revised budget, after you get the inclusion initiative established. I will also require regular reports, consistent with our other projects.

"I personally feel the ROI Partners are the answer to some important issues around here. I can't emphasize enough that we all have a lot riding on this. Don't let us down. Do you have any questions for me?"

The president's requirements and expectations reminded Phoenix of something one of her mentors had shared with her a few years ago: "If you have an opportunity to confirm a deal, make sure you get the other party to commit to something extra beyond what you proposed." It was something Phoenix had failed to do with the SVP earlier. But now, based on Phoenix's additional research, there were a few more things she needed the president to do. Now was the time to ask. "I have five things to ask of you," Phoenix said. "First, I think it would be advisable for you to meet periodically with the ROI Partners and encourage some of the other Executive Team Leaders to attend some sessions as well."

The president laughed. "That won't dent our budget too much, will it? Nothing would be more exciting to me than meeting with some of my best and brightest employees. You know, this could be a good leadership development opportunity for the Executive Leadership Team as well."

Phoenix continued. "Good. Second, I would like you to send the invitation to join the ROI Partners to each person after they're selected and to secure the commitment of their bosses to support their participation in the process."

"Yes, I agree that will be an important signal that this is a priority project. That didn't cost much either." He laughed again. "What else?"

"Next, I would like you to advise HR to incorporate some performance criteria on inclusion for each of the ROI Partners. I believe this would be an indication to the ROI Partners that the work they're doing is 'real work' and not extra, voluntary work."

"I can see to that, too. Certainly it's consistent with other major assignments. What else?"

"When positive results happen, I would like you to communicate them to the organization. I don't mean this for personal acknowledgement. I think it will be crucial to the initiative for the entire company to know what our projects are contributing."

"I certainly agree with that. We can communicate your results periodically through all my normal methods."

Phoenix had one more thing on her mind. "Finally, I would like you to let my SVP and me know immediately if there is anything we're not doing correctly."

"I think I can handle that one, too. As you've seen, I'm very direct. Is there anything else?" When Phoenix indicated there was not, he added, "I've gotten off lightly, I think, don't you?" He nodded toward the SVP, who smiled in agreement.

Phoenix was delighted that the president had agreed to all her requirements. They shook hands, and the president left, escorted by the SVP. They engaged in some small talk about a golf outing the following weekend.

When the SVP returned, he said, "Congratulations on a job well done. I was very proud of you. You delivered what I expected." He hesitated a moment then added, "I know you were disappointed in me because you felt I'd abandoned you."

His remark caught Phoenix by surprise. It was true enough, but she hadn't expected it to be put on the table in such a straightforward manner. Though it wasn't an issue anymore, Phoenix acknowledged to him that the thought had crossed her mind.

"I had already been keeping the president and other key leaders in the loop on the proposal. Although they hadn't seen all the details, I kept them informed, so they weren't surprised.

"I had initially planned to co-present but learned at the last minute that this wasn't an appropriate protocol when proposing a major initiative that I would also be sponsoring. As a new member of the executive team, I'm still learning about the nuances of our corporate culture. That was also the reason I didn't participate by asking you questions during the presentation.

"I knew that at some point you'd have to take the ROI Partners out into our organization. You may not think so, but it will be much harder in the real world than with the Executive Leadership Team. Why do you think we are so tough on ideas? Because we're mean-spirited people? No, because we know how tough it is to implement change. Let's be clear about this. Several of the Executive Leadership Team members truly don't get it and don't support the inclusion initiative; however, I am committed to giving them time to get on board. That will be largely dependent upon the results you achieve. Your ROI Partners will have to stand on their own merit. We have a responsibility to generate profits for our share-holders, create great products for our customers, and maintain a good work environment for our employees.

"I had absolute faith and confidence in your ability to deliver the presentation. I believe in you and the ROI Partners. You'll need to learn to trust me—and others, too!

"As I told you before, the right people are the best resource. For this reason, I was comfortable leaving the meeting early. I wanted to contact you and tell you all this before I left, but I didn't have time. And I made a promise to my family that I'd leave business behind when we left for our vacation. I felt compelled to honor that commitment to my family. I apologize if this caused you any undue stress."

"No problem," Phoenix said. She was immensely relieved. She'd been so busy feeling sorry for herself she hadn't considered there might be some logical reasons why things had happened as they did. "I'm sure that as we continue to work together, we'll become more familiar with each other's unique needs and more comfortable with our relationship, and we'll develop more trust as a consequence. In fact, we'll be practicing the inclusion principles we want to teach others."

"I'm sure we will," the SVP said.

They talked through the next steps for getting the Best People and preparing them to do the work. Phoenix was flying now at new heights, all instruments in working order. She was energized and enthusiastic.

As Phoenix left the meeting, many thoughts rolled around in her head. She had developed a tremendous respect for her SVP. She was learning about integrity from the man's straightforward-ness and trustworthiness. Phoenix felt a bit guilty that she'd enter-tained so many negative thoughts about him, the president, and the Executive Leadership Team. She had succumbed to her own ten-dency to stereotype her leaders. She vowed never again to refer to them as the "Infinite Nine." One thing was certain; Phoenix was learning something about her own personal style and how she reacted to the stress of challenges and changes.

The Executive Leadership Team members had done what she'd asked of them. They'd accepted their "moment of truth" on inclusion.

They'd accepted the commitment to own the process. The questions they'd asked had not been negative. It was their way of being actively involved and processing the information. Everyone, even leaders, had a right to learn, grow, and debate. Inclusion applied to them, too. Phoenix was learning firsthand about the process of inclusion. Sometimes you just had to trust the process and give people the benefit of the doubt. Perhaps her enlightenment in this area would help her as she onboarded others.

Phoenix had learned another important lesson today. Be careful what you ask for because you might get it. The ROI Partners were becoming a reality, and Phoenix was leading the team!

When Phoenix left work that evening, she wanted a change of scenery, so she went for a walk in the park. It was refreshing to be in the open air and to reflect on what she'd learned about herself and the leadership role. She saw herself transforming, being reborn as a new type of leader. She was the *phoenix*!

The phoenix gathered the egg of myrrh and wrapped it in aromatic leaves. Then it began to fly toward the rising sun. The three hundred and sixty varieties of birds gathered round again. By this time, the phoenix had become used to its solitude again and did not want the other birds to accompany it. But it remembered the emperor and his hunters and the way the birds had flapped their wings and cried to help it escape.

CHAPTER SIXTEEN

BEST PEOPLE (PROCESS)

It was time to execute the Phoenix Principles—to take them off the paper and breathe life into them. To that end Phoenix set up a progress meeting with his mentors to solicit their input.

Positioning the Best People was the essential first step of the ROI Partners, and his mentors agreed. Phoenix had six months to identify, onboard, and educate some of the best and brightest, diverse talent in the company to be a part of his team.

"First things first," the VP of marketing and communications said. "Phoenix, you will need to clearly define the type of person who will be involved with the ROI Partners, the qualities and qualifications you want in a team member, and what his or her role should be."

Phoenix had a strong vision of the ROI Partners practicing principles of inclusion with bottom-line business results. "My team," Phoenix replied, "will have a reputation as the best talent in the organization. One day the ROI Partners will have a waiting list of talented people who want to participate."

"That's a worthy goal," said the VP of sales, nodding her approval.

Phoenix had been amazed while doing his research at how little active thought had been given to the selection of the Best People in many organizations for corporate-led inclusion initiatives. Some organizations assigned people strictly on a demographic basis. Others selected people who made a lot of noise about being a part of inclusion. And then there were the horror stories about people who didn't know why they were involved or what they were supposed to do.

"Choosing my team is the most important decision I'll be making," Phoenix said to his mentors. "I need to spend sufficient time on team member selection."

"The best people for choosing the Best People are in HR," the VP of marketing and communications said. "Why don't you let them help?"

The VP of sales agreed to put Phoenix in touch with the SVP of human resources that very day.

Over the next few weeks, Phoenix found it relatively easy to partner with HR to develop and administer a process to select the Best People. The SVP of HR assigned a team, and together with Phoenix they structured the framework. It was a very positive experience for Phoenix. Unlike his previous research, he did not have to do this part alone.

First, Phoenix and the HR team focused on the qualities required for membership in the ROI Partners. The tangible attributes were behaviors or competencies that had been proven in the work history. The successful candidate would be a documented high performer, an effective strategist, a proven influencer, a good learner, and a patient teacher. S/he would be team oriented, action oriented, focused on outcome, and self-motivated. The intangible assets were more about attitude than performance, and were less easy to categorize or measure. The right candidate was passionate but not overly zealous, inspirational to others, capable of motivating a team, energizing, and respected by peers and superiors. The sensitivity of the work would require them to perform with integrity.

Also, Phoenix and HR felt it was very important to seek out as full a range of diversity as possible to be represented by the ROI Partners. They utilized the Diversity Circle to provide them with options to consider: thinking styles and analytical abilities in the mental section; then gender, race, and age in the physical section; and finally those aspects listed in the occupational section.

In addition to some of the standard HR tools commonly used at Xine-Ohp, Phoenix worked with HR to develop a scoring process and an application tool to be used specifically in the selection process. HR helped Phoenix develop a position description for the ROI Partners in the same format as all other job descriptions, something Phoenix hadn't seen during his research.

Next they developed an organizational structure for the ROI Partners with role descriptions and responsibilities. These— organizational structure, member roles, and responsibilities—were working plans that would evolve over time as needs changed. They thought an initial membership size of ten to thirteen would be manageable. The members would have to be willing to commit 10%–20% of their time over twelve to twen-

TANGIBLE ASSETS
- High performers
- Committed
- Team oriented
- Strategist
- Action oriented
- Influencer
- Learner
- Teacher
- Outcome focused
- Self-motivated

INTANGIBLE ASSETS
- Passionate
- Inspirational
- Motivating
- Energizing
- Respected

ty-four months to the project, an agreement that would have to be confirmed by their managers. The terms would be staggered for the sake of continuity. As seasoned members left, they would be replaced by new people. Members would have to agree to attend mandatory team meetings and would be required to participate in one or more committees and subcommittees.

Phoenix and the HR team developed an orientation process for the new ROI Partners that was flexible but structured enough to ensure the members could take up their roles quickly. They would be mentored in the areas of the business, inclusion, the team, their own roles, and, of course, the five Phoenix Principles. The learning process for inclusive leadership was organized in terms of strategy, commitment, and execution model.

After developing the selection process and time line, Phoenix and the HR team assembled a selection committee to conduct the initial interviews and work in triads to administer the selection process. "I want to provide everyone with as much information as possible, in advance, to avoid confusion and vagueness," Phoenix said. He wished to spare others the uncertainties he'd suffered when he started the assignment. They decided that all candidates would be given the selection process information in advance. Potential candidates would also receive letters from the president, with a copy to their bosses, inviting them to apply. Interested candidates would need approval from their bosses to participate. Then the candidates would be provided with a modified overview of Phoenix's presentation of the ROI Partners plan for their review. The document had been revised and authorized by the Executive Leadership Team. All prospective team members would have to sign a confidentiality agreement because of the sensitivity of the data.

"We also need to make it clear that all information provided is a draft and subject to change later by the ROI Partners or the Executive Leadership Team. As we achieve our goals, our priorities will certainly change," Phoenix said. The HR team agreed. They suggested that potential candidates should be encouraged to share their perspectives in writing as well as provide a written essay on why they felt they would make an exceptional ROI Partner.

"That's a good plan," Phoenix agreed. "We need to position the ROI Partners as a prestigious assignment. Prospective candidates should know it's important to their careers to be considered and that it's an honor to be selected."

"To be successful," a member of the HR team proposed, "it will be essential for candidates to understand that being an ROI Partner is a high-priority assignment and that while Phoenix may be the team's leader, they serve at the pleasure of the president."

"And that selected candidates will be subject to final approval by Phoenix and the SVP of operations, in proxy for the president," another HR team member added.

Phoenix and HR agreed that the candidates would have to compete for spots. Competition, already distinctly a part of Xine-Ohp's culture, would ensure that the quality of the candidates would be higher and that, once selected, they would more quickly take ownership of the process.

BENEFITS FOR LEADERS
- Better business results
- New ways to engage top talent
- Improved retention
- New ideas and innovation
- Opportunity to identify future leaders and develop bench strength
- Opportunity to test new ideas and concepts
- Increased communication among departmental silos and other functions

"To get candidates to compete and their bosses to approve, the benefits of participating on the ROI Partners will have to be clear," Phoenix said, thinking out loud. One of his team members responded, "Most people look for professional and personal benefits.

Candidates and their bosses will, too. It's only natural." With that in mind, Phoenix and his HR team developed a preliminary list of benefits. Executives and functional leaders would benefit from better business results, new ways to engage top talent, improved retention, new ideas and innovation, the opportunity to identify future leaders and develop bench strength, the opportunity to test new ideas and concepts, and increased efficiency through better communication among departmental silos and other functions. The ROI Partners would have greater access to leaders. They would have opportunities to network with other high-performing employees and develop reciprocal relationships in which value is both given and received. In developing a broader perspective of the organization and its emerging issues, they would have a chance to develop and demonstrate their own leadership potential and find ways to make a real difference to Xine-Ohp and build their own legacies.

Next, Phoenix and his HR team considered how to establish a pipeline of new members. Phoenix had heard some war stories from other companies about the difficulty of keeping a pool of candidates available. He wanted to minimize that problem. With that in mind, he made a suggestion to the team. "In the event that more qualified candidates are identified than needed, those not selected could be notified that they will be called upon should a position open up in six months or less. Also, the expertise of

BENEFITS FOR ROI PARTNERS
- More access to leaders
- Better business results
- Challenging opportunities
- Networking opportunities with other great employees
- Opportunities to develop reciprocal relationships
- A broader perspective of the organization and its emerging issues
- A chance to make a difference and build a legacy
- A chance to demonstrate leadership potential

those interested but rejected for whatever reason could possibly be used in some capacity related to the ROI Partners' goals."

The team decided, also, that those not selected should be told specifically why. They would be advised that, if they desired to participate, they would be included in a pool of internal resources whose expertise would be called upon. In this way, everyone interested could be included. Phoenix suggested a motto: "Everyone who is competent, passionate, and committed is included." The HR team decided to call these potential resources the ROI

Resource Network. As these people worked with the ROI Partners, they would be in the pipeline of candidates for future terms.

At last, this part of Phoenix's planning was finished. He and the selection committee were ready to start the interviewing and selection process. In fact, Phoenix had worked with several people in HR who would be great additions to the ROI Partners. He hoped they would consider themselves as candidates.

Phoenix appreciated the tremendous support HR was providing. They were all so pleased with the selection process that they shared it with other teams across the organization. The sharing of their inclusive selection process with other teams was the first deliverable for the ROI Partners—even before they had officially formed! Phoenix made a note of it.

As Phoenix reflected on the whole of the work he'd done so far, he was glad he'd begun this inclusion journey. He'd learned so much—not only about inclusion but also about what was involved in exceptional leadership and teamwork. And then something struck him for the first time. As the leader of his new team of ROI Partners, *he* was going to be one of the Best People.

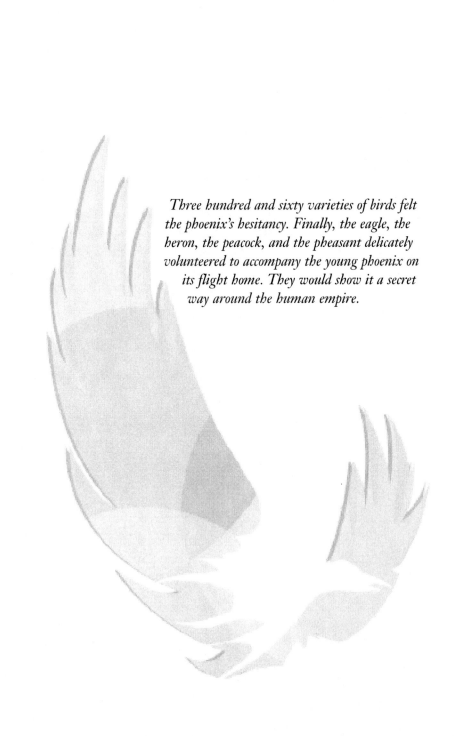

Three hundred and sixty varieties of birds felt the phoenix's hesitancy. Finally, the eagle, the heron, the peacock, and the pheasant delicately volunteered to accompany the young phoenix on its flight home. They would show it a secret way around the human empire.

CHAPTER SEVENTEEN

BEST PEOPLE
(SELECTION)

The selection process was such a monumental task that Phoenix soon realized why many companies didn't do it. It was just plain hard work. There was no glory in it. But she couldn't move forward without it.

THE PHOENIX PRINCIPLES
- **The Best People**
- Compelling Purpose
- Strategic and Measurable Actions
- Solid Infrastructure
- Structured Renewal

During the selection process, she met a diverse group of people from the organization and was amazed at the talent that existed at Xine-Ohp. An incredible number of talented people of varied colors, backgrounds, avenues of expertise, and tenure wanted to contribute to the success of the company. Phoenix and her selection committee identified some people who were achieving fantastic results. There were others who could have done great things but were not in jobs that maximized their talents. The majority were outstanding people with realized and unrealized potential.

Early in the search process, Phoenix and HR recognized that this project had another important side benefit. They were interviewing fifty of the best people in the company in all functions, departments, and regions of the country. The interviews were providing some valuable anecdotal and qualitative insights into the company and its culture, what worked well and what didn't. They were able to identify some key trends. As a result, HR developed an additional questionnaire they used during the confidential interviews and then compiled the resulting information. The results of the research were so insightful regarding the thoughts and viewpoints of top talent that they shared the findings with the SVP of HR, who ultimately shared it with the Executive Leadership Team. The report became known as the "Pulse Report." They decided to make it an annual report to supplement the employee opinion survey.

The Pulse Report had identified several cost containment ideas that might save the company about $500,000 per year. This kind of data was exactly what Phoenix needed to confirm the benefit of the ROI Partners' work for the company. Because of the interviews, two high-potential employees who were on the verge of leaving Xine-Ohp for competing companies were pleased to be transferred to other departments and thereby retained. This was the equivalent of another $200,000 return on investment to the company.

Provided the $500,000 idea worked and the key employees were retained long term, the ROI Partners may have already contributed their second and third deliverables with a potential savings of $700,000, and the team had not even been formed yet!

As planned, the interview process surfaced new ideas and thoughts on the ROI Plan. Phoenix was pleased with the level of engagement of the candidates and with the ideas they were discussing. She captured the information so it could be used in future meetings of the ROI Partners.

Phoenix and the selection committee reviewed the candidates for ROI Partners. The initial tally was five candidates who opted out of the process, seven candidates who were deemed not ready, eight candidates who were considered not ready now but perhaps in the future, twelve candidates who were identified as ready now but couldn't participate because of other commitments or lack of support from their leaders, and eighteen candidates who were considered ready now.

The selection committee reviewed all information carefully and conducted in-depth second- and third-round interviews with each of the eighteen ready-now candidates. The interviews were exciting and informative. After the interviews, they moved one of the candidates to the "ready now but can't because of other commitments" category because the candidate had recently been assigned to another high-priority project that would require all of her time. Phoenix regretted this because she felt the candidate was stellar. But the ROI Partners initially required a commitment of up to twenty-four months, and they needed people who were not only high performers but also had space in their busy schedules.

Two candidates were moved to the "not ready now but perhaps in the future" category. Both candidates were unbelievably talented. But one was not deemed a good team player and might not work well in a collaborative environment. While this candidate was quite successful personally, the selection committee didn't consider her a good initial team member. The other candidate was brilliant, but he had some personal diversity agendas about which he seemed very concerned. Phoenix and the selection committee felt it wouldn't be productive for the ROI Partners if he participated. It was a tough decision for Phoenix because she was hopeful that her own diversity lens was not giving her a fuzzy view. She approved the decision only after much reflection and soul searching.

Phoenix met with her SVP to present the candidates and her own recommendations. After a healthy dialogue that some might have called a debate, the selection committee moved two more of the candidates to the "ready now but can't because of other commitments" category. This left thirteen candidates for the first ROI Partners.

An unlucky number, Phoenix thought, and she then stopped herself, realizing that thinking of thirteen as an unlucky number was a cultural belief. Maybe in some cultures, thirteen was lucky number. There it is, Phoenix thought: diversity and inclusion in action.

The selection committee drafted offer letters to the candidates, and the president sent them out with copies to their bosses. Twelve accepted, and one declined, requesting to be considered again in the future.

The selection committee also sent letters to all the candidates who had either opted out of the process or were considered "not ready now." They were thanked for their participation. Those the selection committee rejected were invited to discuss the decision with Phoenix.

Several candidates accepted the offer. The conversations were tough but necessary. In addition to specific reasons she discussed with them, these rejected candidates just didn't seem to have the required enthusiasm, no real fire for the project. She didn't question their competency, but their passion and commitment were so obviously lacking. Perhaps they would have an opportunity in the future to learn about these qualities, as she had. Maybe some event in their own lives would increase their fire.

One of the meetings was with the individual whom Phoenix had rejected because of his personal diversity agenda. This person was vocal and immovable on some aspects of diversity. After the conversation, Phoenix knew the selection committee had made the right decision for the ROI Partners. But she also felt that this was a person who had potential, and she wanted to know him better, so they agreed to keep in touch.

Invitations went out to "not ready now but perhaps in the future" and those "ready now but have other commitments" to become part of the ROI Resource Network. Nearly a dozen candidates responded that they would like to become part of it. Phoenix included them in a database and planned to maintain a connection with them by contacting them periodically. Role clarity for the network would be developed later.

The candidates who did not respond at all were removed from Phoenix's list.

At the end of the process, HR and Phoenix administered a brief but thorough online survey about the search process to get feedback from all fifty participants. They received a healthy response rate and were very pleased. The feedback was generally favorable, and there were several good suggestions that would be incorporated in the future. Because Phoenix believed in quality control and continuous improvement, performance surveys would always be a standard part of the inclusion process.

In middle of the afternoon on Friday, Phoenix leaned back in her chair with twelve files of the Best People in the company spread out across her desk. They were a diverse group of experienced and talented leaders. Including Phoenix, there were thirteen ROI Partners. An unlucky number? Absolutely not! Thirteen was a *lucky* number. These thirteen individuals were about to make major changes in their company and improve its bottom line by millions of dollars.

Phoenix looked out her window and saw the sun shining brightly in a cloudless sky. On impulse, she decided to leave early. Though she was looking forward to starting her plans for onboarding the team, she was tired. She'd been working hard the past few weeks. She needed to do something fun on the weekend and get some rest, too. The onboarding plans could wait until Monday. She'd start again, renewed, at the beginning of the week.

As the phoenix flew up toward the midday sun, it became more brilliant, and its companions became more timid at the sight of its luminous body. "Do not be afraid," the phoenix told them.

CHAPTER EIGHTEEN

BEST PEOPLE
(ONBOARDING)

After spending two months selecting the Best People, Phoenix had four months left to make his ROI Partners operational. He had kept in touch with them since their selection, and they were enthusiastic and ready to go.

THE PHOENIX PRINCIPLES
- **The Best People**
- Compelling Purpose
- Strategic and Measurable Actions
- Solid Infrastructure
- Structured Renewal

Phoenix's mentor, the VP of sales, advised him that his first priority was to form them into a team and get them aligned on key principles and processes. "Alignment is important for any team," he said, "especially for this group of diverse and highly talented individuals. Like thoroughbred horses, they'll be ready to bolt from the starting gate. You can't allow them to get too far ahead of themselves. It will be necessary to teach them the value of establishing a solid footing so they can make contributions rapidly."

Phoenix thought about the challenge that lay before him. "We should ascertain their alignment with small actions before tackling any major tasks."

"Yes," the VP of sales said. "I think you understand. These people will be ultimately responsible for generating millions of dollars in revenue."

Phoenix had a feeling that this seemingly simple goal of orienting his team would be a monumental task. How would he achieve it? He'd heard that there were consulting companies that specialized in diversity and inclusion. He wondered whether one of them could help with the ROI Partners' onboarding process. Phoenix shared this idea with his mentors, HR, and his SVP. They all concurred, and HR provided Phoenix with the names of some potential firms to interview and agreed to help with the process.

Phoenix researched these companies, along with some others he found on the Internet. He learned quickly that a great number of companies did diversity and inclusion work. They ranged in size from the small one-person or two-person consulting shops to the larger international practices. He thumbed through an article he found that provided some suggestions on how to select a firm. Primarily it advised him to consider how long the firm had been in existence, experience with companies of Xine-Ohp's size, record of success, alignment with his plans, references, personal connection, and pricing.

Phoenix chose candidate firms who met the criteria and, with HR's help, did extensive reviews. They initially interviewed them by phone and then met with several firms in preliminary face-to-face meetings. Phoenix made a point of calling their references. He narrowed his choice to three firms.

Phoenix and HR prepared a scope-of-work document to outline the services he'd expect. HR helped him conduct formal interviews with the three firms. One of his mentors also volunteered to assist in the interview process. After the interviews, one firm stood out, and Phoenix recommended it to his SVP. The critical deciding factors were that this consulting partner had a proven track record of success, was focused on results and measurements, and had a great understanding of the dynamics of corporate culture. The SVP provided some additional thoughts with regard to the services and scope of work. Then after some negotiations with the selected firm, a contract for services was developed. The consulting firm would support Phoenix for the next few months to get the ROI Partners up and running successfully. If necessary, they would be retained on an as-required basis for other specific services and resources.

The new consulting partner had significant experience in inclusion and was impressed with Phoenix's approach. "It's extremely rare to see so much careful forethought in place for an inclusion strategy," the consulting partner said. "You've done half the work for me."

In their first session, Phoenix and his consulting partner agreed that most teams go through a typical process of transforming from a group of talented people into a productive team. The ROI Partners needed to get to the productive stage in four short months because the high-profile assignment would require rapid success. And Phoenix was intensely aware that his own future was still on the line.

The consulting partner suggested a retreat to onboard the members quickly. Phoenix agreed, though he felt "retreat" was a misnomer because it implied going backward or retiring from activity. He and the ROI Partners were looking to the future, not the past. He wanted his team to be the most innovative and for-ward-thinking team at Xine-Ohp. And they certainly weren't going to retreat unnoticed. Phoenix decided he would call their initial off-site orientation a "Forward."

Phoenix and the consulting partner discussed the design of the Forward in relation to the goals Phoenix wanted to achieve. The consulting partner's strategy included the previously discussed need for the team to bond early and build a common purpose. The consulting partner mentioned that the common purpose would also require them to create a common language around the subject of inclusion. When that was accomplished, Phoenix and the consulting partner would answer key questions. Then the team would create their own rules of engagement, gain absolute clarity on the assignment, and learn to own the outcomes.

The consulting partner assured Phoenix that time would be allowed for active debate and dialogue on various aspects of diversity, especially those that often elicited strong emotional responses, such as race, gender, sexual orientation, etc. Sufficient time must be given to discuss individual diversity and inclusion issues and concerns. Real and robust conversations would help the

> **POTENTIAL PITFALLS OF DYSFUNCTIONAL INCLUSION TEAMS**
> - No commitment, no influence
> - No focus, no purpose
> - No infrastructure, no sustenance
> - No measures, no importance
> - No renewal, no relevance

members begin or accelerate their own inclusion journeys. Phoenix wanted some transparent dialogue that was not clouded by political correctness. When the ROI Partners walked away from their onboarding, they needed to understand exactly what they had signed up to do.

Phoenix wanted to make sure each team member was fully equipped to assess the performance of the ROI Partners. It was essential to create a mechanism that would allow diagnostics based on each of the five elements of the Phoenix Principles. He would offer them the benefit of his research on diversity initiatives in other companies. Phoenix wanted each team member to understand that there were really no precedents for where they were going.

Phoenix also felt the ROI Partners should be knowledgeable about the potential pitfalls of their work. To build a confident, high-performing team likely to have influence with the company, they must always assemble the team from committed and respected employees. If not, they would be ineffective. The team must also have a clearly defined focus, or they wouldn't have purpose. Additionally, their purpose must be mutually owned, or their focus would wander and they would end up confused and frustrated. Teams needed infrastructure—something often lacking—to sustain their initiatives. Communication was a vital part of the infrastructure; without it, they couldn't build trust or address "real" issues. Teams needed measures and expectations, or they would generate trivial work. And, without consistent renewal, they could become insular, stale, redundant, and ultimately irrelevant.

In short, the ROI Partners would need a complete understanding of each of the five elements to make their initiative successful.

Best People	**Strategist**: Influential, learning focused, strategic, teacher and/or influencer, understands diversity and inclusion, understands the business and culture. **Committed**: Highly self-motivated; passionate and committed to self, others, and the company; inspirational; motivating; and energizing. **Action Oriented**: High performer, team oriented, results oriented, adaptive to change, role model for others.
Compelling Purpose	Aligned with business objectives of organization (the ROI five-year growth plan) and focused on return on invest-

ment, vision, mission, aligned end state, diversity, and inclusion clarity.

Strategic and Measurable Actions	Aligned with compelling purpose, measurable results, strategic interventions, ROI, critical few focus, cultural alignment.
Solid Infrastructure	Organizing infrastructure, resource availability, common language, shared practices and values, organizational support.
Structured Renewal	Transformation, rejuvenation, continuous learning, leadership rotation, accountability, valuing differences, fun.

Phoenix intended to spend a substantial amount of time in the Forward on the ROI Plan that he'd developed. He wanted to get the team's thoughts on the plan and to make important modifications based on their input.

There would be pre-work and post-meeting assignments.

He also wanted to make sure there would be a high level of interactivity during the meeting and time for the members to share their commitment with each other. It was important for them to enter into a contract with each other and build rapport.

And, finally, Phoenix wanted them to have fun.

It was a tall order, but the consulting partner promised her company could deliver the results.

In preparation for the time after the Forward, when he would have to transfer the ownership of this project from himself to the ROI Partners, Phoenix invited the president and the SVP of operations to have the same challenging dialogue and debate with his team as he had once had. Both executives had agreed to participate and to provide an unprecedented three hours of time on the last day of the Forward. In fact, the president had also convinced two of the other Executive Leadership Team members to attend, both of whom had expressed skepticism. Phoenix predicted the dialogues would not be any easier for the team than they had been for him. The big difference was that the ROI Partners would be challenged as a group; its members would not have to defend their objectives and methods alone as he had.

The consulting partner worked with Phoenix to develop and frame the desired outcomes, agenda, exercises, and logistics. They decided the Forward would take at least three days, so they planned for three and a half days. Every nuance was considered. Every idea was debated. All the materials were developed. The consulting partner provided some of her company's unique tools that would neatly accomplish some of Phoenix's objectives. Everything was done within the protocol and norms of Xine-Ohp's culture, with a bit of innovation in several important places.

This Forward was a high-stakes meeting, and Phoenix knew it. The expertise and calmness of his consulting partner helped ease his mind. This consulting partner had done this kind of thing many times before. Phoenix felt he'd made a good choice and was comfortable with it.

As the phoenix flew into the sun, it grew larger
and flew higher. Its companions became nervous,
swooping lower. At last the phoenix grew so large
that it blocked the sun altogether, causing a great
shadow to fall on the earth. The phoenix itself
appeared as a black egg ringed by fire. The
other birds trembled in fear. "The phoenix
has swallowed up the sun!" they
exclaimed. "No!" said the phoenix. And
to prove it, it flew past the sun and
became the jewel-hued
phoenix once again,
shimmering in the
dazzling light of
the sun.

CHAPTER NINETEEN

BEST PEOPLE (FORWARD)

When Phoenix arrived for the Forward, everything was well in place. The consulting partner and her team had arrived the night before and set up everything with the help of Phoenix's new administrative assistant, who also had been very helpful in coordinating the

> **THE PHOENIX PRINCIPLES**
> - **The Best People**
> - Compelling Purpose
> - Strategic and Measurable Actions
> - Solid Infrastructure
> - Structured Renewal

logistics. Phoenix's mentors had come through for her again as well. They had secured additional staff from HR and one person from communications.

Phoenix had arranged for a variety of special presentations throughout the session.

People were moving with purpose and precision, like musicians performing a master concert. Phoenix definitely appreciated the experience of her consulting partner. Her calm competence relieved some of Phoenix's pent-up anxiety from the past few days. Phoenix kept reminding herself to trust the process, but that was easier said than done. She felt her career hanging in the balance. If this session bombed, she would be bombing out in front of some of the most influential people in the company, including the president, the Executive Leadership Team, and the SVP of operations.

As the ROI Partners arrived, Phoenix was excited. They were some of the best and brightest people in the company. They were a highly diverse group representing all aspects of the sections in the Diversity Circle. They represented a cross section of Xine-Ohp's functions: sales, marketing, HR, research, legal, operations, finance, and others. They came from different parts of the world. With their unique backgrounds and experiences, they were as diverse on the inside as on the outside. They seemed confident, friendly, focused, and highly intelligent.

In fact, the team had a level of intensity that reminded Phoenix of the Executive Leadership Team. In them, she saw that same passion, commitment, and dedication to the success of the company. These were the future leaders of Xine-Ohp, the "heirs apparent" to the twenty-fifth floor. They represented the interests of the current employees, customers, and shareholders of Xine-Ohp, and held its future in their hands.

Phoenix felt as if something magical was about to happen. She'd lit a fire for the company, and it was burning brightly!

When the meeting was called to order, Phoenix introduced the consulting partner, who framed the objectives for the next few days. Even the breaks, dinner, and scheduled free times were designed to achieve specific learning and teaming outcomes. The agenda was divided into three parts: strategy, commitment, and execution. She established the session's guiding principles and advised everyone that, while the outcomes were non-negotiable, the agenda was flexible. There was real work to be done. Then she collected a survey that had been included in the pre-work packages.

Next, the consulting partner engaged the participants in an exercise designed to relax them and get their commitment for full participation. The overall plan for the Forward contained a balance of interactive and reflective activities.

After the introductory exercise, the consulting partner focused on the strategy part of the agenda, starting with a detailed presentation from Phoenix on the history of the project, followed by its objectives and responsibilities. While the participants had heard much of this before, Phoenix spent a significant amount of time making sure she was consistent in sharing what she'd learned from her research on best practices. Many questions and answers followed. Those questions that could not be answered were placed in a "parking lot" to hold until answers could be found. This became the standard practice for all unanswered questions.

Several invited presenters from finance, marketing, sales, and research spoke on some of the emerging challenges, trends, and opportunities for Xine-Ohp. The ROI five-year growth plan was dissected in detail. The participants fired questions at the speakers similar to the ones Phoenix had received from the Executive Leadership Team and her SVP. It was obvious that this team had done their homework.

Phoenix then spent time helping the ROI Partners understand the initial ROI Plan. They were invited to discuss it, debate it, support it, or tear it up and start all over again if they felt that was needed. A robust dialogue centered on the principles of inclusion. While there still wasn't a common working definition for inclusion, there was sufficient alignment to make a beginning.

They held some small-group dialogues, which were intended to help the ROI Partners agree on a Compelling Purpose. They struggled a bit because they had not yet come together as a cohesive team. They were still individuals asking questions and providing input. But the dialogue was good, and the information shared would be useful in future meetings.

The day ended with a highly interactive, insightful, and fun activity on thinking style diversity. The dynamics of the individuals gave Phoenix an idea of how the ROI Partners might interact as a team. The process of acquiring a common experience and language had begun. Some great dinner activities and evening meetings followed.

The next day the consulting partner changed the focus to the commitment part of the agenda. This was designed to help the team bond into a unit. Some of the pre-work activity was used to gain deeper insights into each member's personal goals and struggles. There was a significant amount of conversation around what they needed from the team, the company, and the process to carry the work forward. Participants were permitted to share personal information at a level that was comfortable for them.

Additionally, the consulting partner led the participants through some deep and insightful conversations regarding various diversity and inclusion principles, practices, and dialogues. The conversations were direct with no holds barred. At times they were tense and confrontational, but the consulting partner was able to lead the participants to the higher concepts the conversations were intended to promote. Because the Best People were selected, the process was easier than it might have been with another group.

The consulting partner ended this part of the agenda with two interactive presentations, one to teach the principles of trust and another on the guidelines for productive communication. These two items were an essential part of the Solid Infrastructure.

The agenda for the third day centered on execution. First, each team member developed a personal inclusion plan. Each one paired with another team member for mutual support. Then they reviewed the Best People, Compelling Purpose, Strategic and Measurable Actions, Solid Infrastructure, and Structured Renewal success principles and established each of the five principles as a basic committee. Each team member chose a committee to lead or co-chair and on which he or she would concentrate.

Frank, a member of Xine-Ohp's strategic planning team, was a natural to chair the Compelling Purpose Committee. He'd been with the company for twenty years. He invited Regina to co-chair the committee with him. Regina, in her early thirties and originally from France, had come into the organization when Xine-Ohp bought her company four years ago. She had previous experience with corporate change initiatives.

Robert, a new-timer from the controller's department, volunteered to lead the Strategic and Measurable Actions Committee with Diane, an engineer from quality management. Robert had recently come to Xine-Ohp from a casino on the East Coast of the United States, and Diane had background in the auto industry in Germany. They were both analytical and detail oriented. They asked LaShawna to join them because of her expertise in data management.

Xine-Ohp's Chief of Logistics, Sonja, had some definite ideas about how the Solid Infrastructure would work and decided that chairing this committee would be her last big project before retiring from Xine-Ohp in a few years. She chose Luis, an administrative services manager, to be her co-chair. Luis, originally from South America, also had extensive experience in computer technology. Lee Song, a welcome associate from marketing and communications, rounded out this committee.

The Structured Renewal Committee was headed by Darla, an African who had a Ph.D. in organizational development. She had an excellent training team whose services could be called upon by the ROI Partners. From sales there was Keenan, who was a paraplegic and did a lot of motivational speaking; he co-chaired this Phoenix Principle for the ROI Partners.

Phoenix was truly grateful to turn over the Best People Committee to Sally and Dave for further improvement of its processes, selection, and orientation. Sally was recommended because of her expertise in HR. As a director of operations, Dave was a peer of Phoenix and, like Phoenix, had been on several recent leadership rotations where he had made many contacts throughout the company. He had some ideas on the ROI Resource Network concept that would definitely improve it.

In addition, each ROI Partner volunteered for at least two subcommittees to be determined later when they had a better idea of what their projects would be and how their resources would need to be divided.

With the other twelve ROI Partners in place as committee leaders and co-chairs, Phoenix realized the inclusion initiative had undergone a significant change. It was no longer *her* project but was being transformed into the work of the ROI Partners. The varied talents and skills of her team would drive the initiative forward from here. And because these committee leaders were respected and influential, the ROI Partners would have few problems persuading other departments to work with them.

Throughout the three days of the Forward, Phoenix and the consulting partner worked together to make the appropriate changes and adjustments, while keeping the meeting's execution seamless and focused on the outcomes. By the end of the third day, the team members' comments made it clear that the Forward was a phenomenal success. Phoenix was thrilled.

Phoenix told her team, "Our only major task remaining is to prepare for the discussion with the president. He will be attending tomorrow's session with several members of his Executive Leadership Team and the SVP of operations." In the past, Phoenix would have still been worried about this meeting. She felt calm now. Because she'd begun to trust the ROI Partners and the Phoenix Principles, she let go of her anxiety.

At the last minute Phoenix made an intuitive decision. She decided the consulting partner would simply observe the next day's meeting. This was a "moment of truth" talk about the future of the company. She also decided that she would take a subdued role, similar to the role her SVP had taken during her own presentation to the Executive Leadership Team. Phoenix needed to confirm what she already believed, that she had indeed chosen the Best People and that they could carry the momentum forward. She announced her decision to the team.

The next day when the meeting with the Executive Team started, Phoenix made a short introduction stating, "I would like to introduce you to the ROI Partners. We are thirteen people who are committed to the short- and long-term financial success of Xine-Ohp, and we are going to help the company make or save millions of dollars by making the company more inclusive." With that, Phoenix outlined the five committees and announced that their leaders and co-chairs would be in charge of the discussions in their pertinent areas. Phoenix stepped back and smiled at her SVP. He immediately understood the silent message and returned the smile.

Two and a half hours later, the conversation was still going strong. Sometimes the debate led to agreement and sometimes to disagreement. There were high points and low points. It was clear to Phoenix that the Best People were at the table. It was clear to the Executive Leadership Team that they had invested in the right project, and it was clear to the ROI Partners team members that their executives were engaged and supportive.

After Phoenix's administrative assistant reminded her that several people had flights to catch, Phoenix started to wind down the meeting and then closed it. She said goodbye to the ROI Partners and her support team. There would, of course, be challenges along the way, but she had the Best People in the company as her partners. For the first time in months, Phoenix was on a team again, and it felt great. They were about to change the company and help it make millions of dollars in revenue or savings.

When everyone had gone, Phoenix went to her laptop and sent a message to the consulting partner, the administrative team, her SVP, the ROI Partners, the Executive Team, and her mentors: *Mission accomplished. We have lift off! Thank you all for your support. We came as the Best People; we left as the Best Team!*

And, of course, she attached a post-meeting survey.

With the Forward behind her and the team formed, the anxiety that had burned inside Phoenix dropped completely away. That night Phoenix fell into the deepest sleep she'd enjoyed since the project had fallen into her lap.

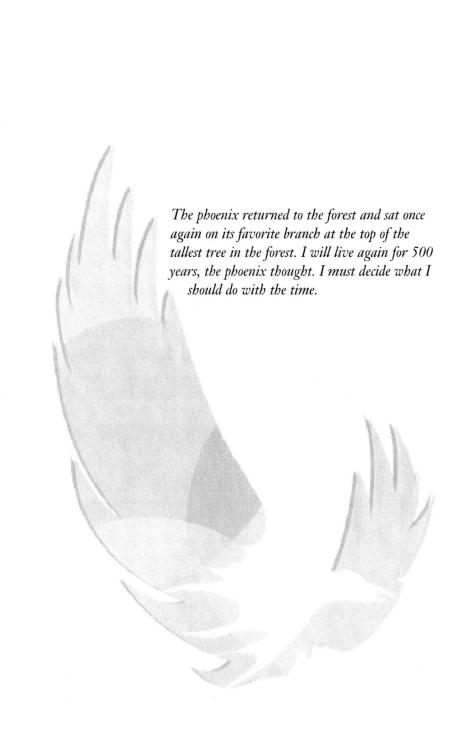

The phoenix returned to the forest and sat once again on its favorite branch at the top of the tallest tree in the forest. I will live again for 500 years, the phoenix thought. I must decide what I should do with the time.

CHAPTER TWENTY

COMPELLING PURPOSE

For the next few days, Phoenix felt fantastic about his accomplishment. Then doubts set in again. He had assembled his team of ROI Partners and oriented them with the Forward. They were achievement-focused,

THE PHOENIX PRINCIPLES
• The Best People
• **Compelling Purpose**
• Strategic and Measurable Actions
• Solid Infrastructure
• Structured Renewal

high performers, ready for action. He was proud that he'd brought them together. But it was up to him to direct them and focus their energy. If he didn't, he'd have a runaway team. A scary thought.

Phoenix immediately arranged a lunch meeting with his mentors. He needed advice again and a lunch check was a small price to pay.

The VP of marketing and communications congratulated him profusely on the success of the Forward.

"You've put together an excellent team," the VP of sales said. "They're ready for action."

"Yes, I know," Phoenix replied.

"What's bothering you, Phoenix?" the VP of sales asked. Not much escaped her.

"There's a lot of unfinished business from the Forward. The ROI Partners have a lot to decide. Getting them together is my next step, but I'm not sure how to channel all this expertise and energy," he admitted. "I'm not sure I know how to harness all of the great ideas. Many of them have much more experience than I do."

"You have the vision, Phoenix. You'll do great," the VP of sales said.

"Thank you," said Phoenix. But he knew it wasn't that simple. And he knew the VP of sales knew it, too.

"Perhaps you should call your Compelling Purpose Committee together first, before you have your first ROI Partners meeting," the VP of marketing and communications suggested.

"That's a good idea," the VP of sales said. "Finalizing your Compelling Purpose may be useful to get things underway."

The relief Phoenix felt was worth the price of many lunches. "Thank you," he told his mentors, grateful they were there to advise him.

As soon as he returned to his office, Phoenix called the Compelling Purpose Committee co-chairs, Frank and Regina, and asked them to meet with him the same day. Phoenix shared information with them on many diversity initiatives he'd researched. While much of the work was good, many of those initiatives had not been tied to an overall strategy or tactics.

"I'm reminded of an old adage," Frank said. "If you don't know where you're going, any road can get you there."

"We need to help Xine-Ohp avoid this pitfall," Regina said.

"We have a great team," Phoenix told them. "The problem is that everyone on the ROI Partners has a lot of ideas on what our purpose is, what we should do, and how to go about it. Too many ideas can be as much of a problem as not having any."

Frank agreed. "Our Compelling Purpose has to be very focused to be successful. It must clearly articulate our mission and strategy."

Phoenix knew that Frank was speaking from his long experience as a strategic planner at Xine-Ohp. Phoenix felt very good about Frank, and Regina, too, because she had some background as a leader of corporate change initiatives.

Frank and Regina looked at the mission statement that Phoenix had previously outlined and agreed that it was good. They made only a few small changes before it was ready to present to the ROI Partners. Their final draft read, *"To leverage the principles of inclusion to achieve measurable strategic and financial results in specifically target-ed areas."*

Over the next few days, Phoenix, Frank, and Regina agreed to an approach similar to one that had been used successfully by some sophisticated diversity departments. They outlined a collaborative strategy that included full participation between the ROI Partners and specific divisions, not mandated by either side. All divisions would be expected to develop their own ROI plans. In general, the ROI Partners would serve as resources and facilitators of the process for the divisions. The executive team and the SVP of each department encouraged this kind of collaboration because they were co-owners with the ROI Partners of the overall inclusion initiative.

One important task they completed early on and reconfirmed with the Executive Leadership Team was a statement of the ROI Partners' scope of authority. This defined the actual power the team had, how they operated, what they controlled, and what their limits were. Phoenix had uncovered many horror stories resulting from a lack of authority, an unclear scope of authority, or misdirected authority. Each ROI Partner must be aware of and buy into the parameters of his or her authority and remain clearly focused on the team's Compelling Purpose. If any doubt arose, the Compelling Purpose Committee and the ROI Partners would work with the Executive Leadership Team to reestablish clarity.

The Compelling Purpose Committee members, understanding that there were limits to the ROI Partners' involvement in Xine-Ohp's business and employee issues, proposed guidelines on what they could and couldn't be involved in. For example, an issue might be a great one, but the timing might not be right, the right leadership might not be in place, or the organization's structure couldn't provide what they needed. Their stated mission and Compelling Purpose would help the ROI Partners make those decisions.

The Compelling Purpose Committee agreed that Phoenix's job was to communicate the team's purpose to the organization. He would also become a facilitator and arbitrator to help all processes run smoothly.

They worked for the next several weeks to identify the areas where they could have the greatest impact. The main prerogative was that their Compelling Purpose had to be connected directly to the ROI five-year growth plan. This document was Xine-Ohp's "tablet of stone," outlining its organizational goals for the future.

They combined efforts with the other ROI Partners to do some initial research throughout the organization to determine the best approaches for implementing the principles of inclusion. They started by planning some pre-work in the form of questionnaires and interviews to understand the current challenges and opportunities in each function and in the organization at large. Their Compelling Purpose not only had to be linked to the ROI five-year growth plan, but also aligned with other appropriate organizational priorities and initiatives.

After the results of their research were in, Phoenix and the Compelling Purpose Committee discussed them with their consulting partner. The consulting partner mentioned a statistically valid study that provided examples of best practice areas, some of which could be applicable to the ROI Partners' needs. Later, it would be possible to compare their results with these best practice performance standards.

Frank advised them to focus on a few critical areas. "We'll be more successful if we don't try to do too much at once," he advised. "The key is to select our strategic initiatives carefully."

Regina suggested piloting their projects before any large-scale implementation.

"That would be good," Frank agreed. "Pilot programs allow you to make adjustments in your plans for any unexpected complications that arise."

Because of their research, the Compelling Purpose Committee decided to prioritize their actions over the next three years, and the ROI Partners agreed when Frank and Regina presented the strategy to them.

In the first year, they would leverage inclusion to increase sales penetration in high-potential but overlooked markets, improve operational efficiency, and enhance customer service. These goals linked to Xine-Ohp's ROI five-year growth plan in the areas of corporate expansion and enhancing reputation.

In the second year, the Compelling Purpose Committee planned a strategy to leverage inclusion in four areas: to improve the internal environment by enhancing day-to-day interactions between individuals and departments, improve leadership competencies, facilitate the cultural integration process during mergers and acquisitions, and aid innovation by implementing inclusive methods to generate breakthrough ideas. All these strategies linked to the company's ROI five-year plan in the areas of increasing employee retention and development and the growth of new products.

During the third year, the Compelling Purpose Committee would link to Xine-Ohp's ROI five-year plan of living the corporate values, enhancing reputation, and increasing employee retention and development. They would achieve these goals by integrating the principles of inclusion into corporate communications, education, and HR systems and processes.

All strategies would have to be reviewed regularly to ensure alignment with departmental goals and the ROI Partners' Compelling Purpose, with appropriate adjustments made as necessary.

"How will we know our business impact for each project in terms of dollars earned or saved?" one of the ROI Partners asked. "A variety of factors could influence financial results."

"I believe the ROI Partners can develop reliable metrics in conjunction with our partners in other functions," Phoenix replied. "We'll have to do some pre-work for benchmarking purposes and post-work analysis for comparison."

Frank and Regina explained that pre- and post-work analyses would require the ROI Partners and the cooperating divisions to review, participate in, and support various quantitative and qualitative research studies and reviews, including marketing studies, sales projections, employee opinion surveys, efficiency studies, departmental quality studies, new product development, and employee retention analysis. From these kinds of studies and analyses, measures could be established.

The Compelling Purpose Committee also created formal guidelines for implementing and maintaining the ROI Partners' Compelling Purpose. The Compelling Purpose Committee prepared a copy of their plan and other pertinent documents for distribution to the ROI Partners and others as was appropriate.

While the job of the ROI Partners would not be easy, Phoenix was confident they could make their collaborative strategy work. The president and the Executive Leadership Team supported it.

And, because the ROI Partners' strategy focused on business issues and return on investment, the departments, regions, or functions would ultimately be the ones acknowledged and rewarded for successes, thus making them more eager for future collaboration. Word would spread, and then other functions would see the value of working with the ROI Partners.

Through their work together, Phoenix experienced his team's amazing potential for vision, innovation, strategy, commitment, and action. However, with their Compelling Purpose outlined, the real work had only just begun. A huge responsibility lay before them, though it also held vast possibilities.

There are many animals, like the turtle and the serpent, who live close to the ground and get lost easily. There are those, like the deer and the rabbit, who must run from the hunters. With my extraordinary sight, the phoenix thought, I can be their eyes. Just thinking about it caused the phoenix to grow stronger.

CHAPTER TWENTY-ONE

STRATEGIC AND
MEASURABLE ACTIONS

After having developed their Compelling Purpose into a three-year strategy, Phoenix was ready to meet with the Strategic and Measurable Actions Committee: Robert, from the controllers depart-

> **THE PHOENIX PRINCIPLES**
> - The Best People
> - Compelling Purpose
> - **Strategic and Measurable Actions**
> - Solid Infrastructure
> - Structured Renewal

ment; Diane, an engineer and quality expert; and LaShawna, experienced in data management. All were detailed thinkers and data-oriented professionals. They were the perfect team to guide the ROI Partners in selecting actions and measuring their effects on the return on investment. This committee would work closely with specific regions, departments, or functions to achieve the goals of the ROI Partners.

Phoenix began the meeting by referring to diversity initiatives she'd previously researched and to information she'd gathered on why those initiatives had or had not been successful. She reinforced the point that the ROI Partners had to establish the value of their strategic actions, and that value had to be shared with the organization. "If not," she told them, "as you well know, when budget-cutting season comes, initiatives with their values unproven will be sent to the chopping block."

"We must employ actions that are both *strategic* and *measurable*," Diane said.

"Right," Phoenix responded. "Our Compelling Purpose Committee has done a great job of putting us on the right path. As we align our actions with our Compelling Purpose, we have to remember that real solutions at Xine-Ohp will have to be more than just doing some training, creating a more diverse workforce, or promoting a few people. We can't merely change a few policies and hold a few people accountable, though best practices include all those actions."

"It's going to be difficult to measure the ROI in some cases," Robert noted.

"Yes," Phoenix replied. "That's why many companies don't do it."

"It could be hard to get the information and resources to do it effectively," LaShawna said in a worried tone of voice.

"It will be a challenge," Phoenix agreed, "but we have to do it. We can work in conjunction with the Compelling Purpose Committee to choose the actions that have the potential to be the most strategic and provide the biggest impact on the organization."

"Are we assuming those are the actions that would provide the most return on investment?" Robert asked.

"From a quality standpoint that sounds logical," Diane said.

To Phoenix's delight, Robert volunteered for the next important step. "I can work with the team to project some numbers," he said.

Phoenix was pleased with the committee's response. She knew there were bound to be some significant disagreements in the future, but for now this committee was working together smoothly.

To direct them, Phoenix referred them to the study their consulting partner had recommended, which provided examples of best practice areas and how they are implemented and measured. Using this information, over the next few weeks the committee identified some actions consistent with their mission and strategy, and also identified potential functions in the organization with which they might partner for those actions. They drew up a proposal for consideration by the ROI Partners.

Throughout the entire process of getting all the ROI Partners' committees up and running, Phoenix kept the SVP of operations and the president in the loop. These executives were partnering on this work with Phoenix in such a way that she felt she had two more mentors. They continued to have challenging conversations that, while tough, contributed tremendously to Phoenix's professional and personal growth. She also noticed that other ROI Partners were receiving those same benefits from several Executive Leadership Team members and other executives with whom they partnered in various functions.

The SVP of operations demanded budgets for each Strategic Measurable Action they proposed, and the team was prepared. Robert's work in this area was right on target. Good budget management required a detailed written plan for their work with any department, region, or function. LaShawna's data management experience helped considerably in this area.

The president, they found, was not above dropping in on the ROI Partners' general meetings or committee meetings unannounced. He always went a step further than the SVP and asked, "What is your projected ROI for this project?" Phoenix was glad her team had anticipated this question. Diane's logical approach, along with LaShawna's extensive database, was instrumental in pulling all the pieces together to project the return on investment for each project. It was time consuming to collect all the information they needed and project all the numbers, but Phoenix wanted the ROI Partners to operate on sound business principles. In the end, their projected overall ROI was impressive. The president was pleased.

As the Strategic and Measurable Actions Committee worked, they completed another important step for the ROI Partners. Guided by their Compelling Purpose and using the knowledge gained in their experience, Phoenix and the ROI Partners created for future use formal guidelines for creating Strategic and Measurable Actions and for prioritizing them.

Strategically, their actions would focus on the critical areas they'd outlined and prioritized for their Compelling Purpose. Each action would need a designated process

**INFRASTRUCTURE REQUIRE-
MENTS FOR STRATEGIC AND
MEASURABLE ACTIONS**
- Designated process owner
- Internal support
- Sufficient funding and resources
- Critical path schedule
- Strategy for analyzing and communicating results

owner, internal support and commitment, a plan for sufficient funding and resources, a critical path schedule, and a strategy for analyzing and communicating results. The guidelines created by the Strategic and Measurable Actions Committee guaranteed that all actions taken would result in a *measurable* ROI. They would also use Xine-Ohp's communications network to distribute a report of the ROI Partners' progress throughout the company on a yearly basis.

According to the Compelling Purpose Committee's outline for their three-year strategy, the Strategic and Measurable Actions would focus during the first year on increasing profit margins. While they couldn't always confine their energies strictly to profits, this was the area where they would gain the most initial success and recognition.

To that end, the Strategic and Measurable Actions Committee planned to increase sales penetration in markets that had largely gone untapped. They would achieve their goals by partnering with sales, marketing and communications, and new product development. Specifically, they would develop and pilot inclusive products, inclusive marketing and promotional materials, and initiate cross-cultural sales training. They would measure increased sales, market penetration, and customer feedback.

Also in the first year, the committee planned actions geared toward improving operational efficiency in cross-functional departments. The Strategic and Measurable Actions Committee and the ROI Partners would partner directly with the SVP of operations, quality control, and other specific functions. Their actions in this area would be to develop inclusive team efficiency sessions and create cross-functional or interregional partnerships. The SVP liked the idea of testing their actions with pilot programs. Their metrics were productivity and quality.

The Strategic and Measurable Actions Committee also included, in this first year, efforts to improve customer service. The ROI Partners would pair with functional teams in legal, HR, operations, and sales. They would develop and pilot new inclusive guidelines, education, and arbitration processes for associate and customer interactions. Then they would pilot mentoring and development processes for "at-risk" associates. The metrics would be retention, development, reputation, and legal exposure.

The president liked the plans and encouraged the ROI Partners to carry out this work.

The Strategic Measurable Actions Committee also outlined a general plan for their second-year priority of improving the internal environment. They would leverage inclusion to improve daily operations, to integrate inclusion principles into the leadership development and onboarding processes, and to facilitate the integration of corporate cultures following business acquisitions. In addition, they considered a corporate-wide quality initiative. Functional partners would include HR, corporate acquisitions, and operations. The metrics for these actions would focus on talent retention, inclusive culture and values, and quality control.

Their third-year strategy for leveraging inclusion in company communications would require them to incorporate inclusion messages in sales brochures, employee newsletters, and the annual report. Metrics would include the quantity and quality of inclusion messages in these communications. Their functional partner would be marketing and communications.

An equally important part of this priority during in the third year was to transfer the principles of inclusion to the corporation at large through Xine-Ohp's educational programs. Their consulting partner was helpful in this area because she was skilled in diversity awareness and skills training, minority recruiting, mentoring methods, and conflict resolution. Inclusion education would be provided at several levels. For leadership, the measurements would take place around leadership development programs and management training. For other associates, the metrics would focus on associate development and inclusive culture and behavior. Their functional partners would be organizational development and HR.

When the ROI Partners and the functional departments with whom they paired had agreed upon all actions, the Strategic and Measurable Actions Committee began benchmarking to establish a baseline before the implementation of any actions. Benchmarking was essential to assess the economic impact of any action or intervention. Current demographics, market conditions, retention rates, and other data would be compared with later studies of the same kind.

Measurements would also have to be taken periodically to prove results and ongoing value. Actions could appear ineffective if results were not reliably analyzed, or if advance preparation and follow-up were hasty or lacking altogether.

While there was some resistance, with people complaining that *everything* couldn't be measured, Phoenix and the Strategic and Measurable Actions Committee knew that, having chosen their strategic actions carefully, clearly defining what could be measured and how to measure it was both necessary and achievable. Xine-Ohp's culture required the metrics. The company would not sustain any process or practice long term unless a rate of return could be directly associated with it. "*What gets measured gets done*" was the Xine-Ohp mantra, and it became the ROI Partners' mantra as well. They planned to validate all actions and priorities on an annual basis.

It was tedious work, but this level of commitment, rigor, and planning was absolutely necessary. Phoenix had read research articles by well-known academicians who had mentioned this lack. Certainly Phoenix's advance work, the talents and expertise of the ROI Partners, and the consulting partner's advice had made the process much easier.

The consulting partner continued to counsel the ROI Partners, and Phoenix was pleased to have her support. At the same time, Phoenix was most pleased with the strategic thinking of the ROI Partners. She was glad that so many good ideas had come from the ROI Partners and their functional teams. Their ideas, experience, and connections helped tremendously. It was amazing what the Best People could accomplish when together they put their minds to work, put their hearts into it, and followed up with definite plans.

Perhaps my friends—the eagle, the heron, the peacock, and the pheasant—would help me look for other creatures who have lost their way, the phoenix thought. I will ask them today.

CHAPTER TWENTY-TWO

SOLID INFRASTRUCTURE

Phoenix worked diligently with the Solid Infrastructure Committee to construct an adequate and reliable infrastructure to support the ROI Partners. The Solid Infrastructure would be an important element for

---
THE PHOENIX PRINCIPLES
- The Best People
- Compelling Purpose
- Strategic and Measurable Actions
- **Solid Infrastructure**
- Structured Renewal
---

success over the long term. Phoenix was sure his committee was equal to the task.

In his initial meeting with the committee, Phoenix likened Solid Infrastructure to the components of an office building. Without a foundation, frame, and support beams, the building couldn't stand. Without rooms, a building couldn't be organized for activities. Without communication lines, an office couldn't carry out its daily work. Without a Solid Infrastructure, the ROI Partners couldn't exist or function either.

"Then, I think top leadership commitment and support is the 'foundation' upon which everything rests," said Sonja, Xine-Ohp's chief of logistics.

"Yes," said Phoenix. "The president and the SVP understand that and are willing to publicly voice commitment for the work. In fact, that's why the ROI Partners report directly to the president. Everyone at Xine-Ohp must understand that top leadership will be actively involved in our work."

The "frame" contained resources such as budgeted funds, administrative support, and technical resources. "My department can certainly help with that," Luis said. Luis came to the ROI

Partners as Xine-Ohp's administrative services manager. "We can work with the Strategic and Measurable Actions Committee to calculate what will be needed."

Lee Song, from marketing and communications, had a brilliant idea. "If we're working with other functions and departments to save them money or increase their revenue, why not find a way to charge expenses to *their* projects and budgets?"

"I couldn't agree more," Phoenix said with a broad smile.

The Solid Infrastructure Committee then discussed innovative ways to charge their expenses to other projects as might be deemed appropriate by the organization. In some cases, it made sense to get resources allocated from other departments and functions. In other cases, they might receive resources directly from the SVP and the president. Of course, they all agreed they would need to manage all their resources as carefully as it was done everywhere else in the company. In certain cases, Phoenix thought, the ROI Partners might actually raise the bar of excellence in resource management.

They also discussed the decision-making processes, which they agreed were the "support beams" that kept them functioning.

"I always thought majority rule is unwise," Luis said. "If 51% is for something and 49% is against, it can't be fair."

"In fact," Sonja added, "that expectation seems counter to the principles of inclusion. Differences exist and should be accepted. If 49% of people feel forced to go along with things they don't agree with, it seems unproductive."

"But it's unrealistic to expect 100% consensus on any issue," Phoenix advised.

Eventually, the Solid Infrastructure Committee agreed on the 80/20 rule for making decisions. When 80% consensus was reached, a decision would be accepted. Those who found themselves in the other 20% must trust the wisdom of the rest of the group and actively support the decision. All major decisions, however, were still subject to review and approval by the president.

The "rooms" of the ROI Partners' infrastructure were the committees through which they organized the work. As the team got up and running, subcommittees would be formed to carry out various aspects of the work.

To function well, it was important for the team to have "communication lines" to the rest of the organization. Unsuccessful diversity initiatives often did not have communication protocols in place, or they weren't practiced. Lee Song was the natural choice to develop this area. His department would work on a plan to announce the rollout of the ROI Partners and handle ongoing communications to Xine-Ohp about their activities and accomplishments.

"Communications among the ROI Partners are important as well," Phoenix told the committee. "I feel good about how we're performing and making connections, but I expect members of this highly diverse team to have a few problems somewhere along the line in understanding each other's various working and thinking styles. People will surely irritate each other sometimes."

The committee discussed Phoenix's concerns and agreed that any incidences would have to be admitted and addressed right away. The team couldn't afford to ignore problems that arose and hope they'd go away. As part of their Solid Infrastructure to make the ROI Partners a high-performing team, an internal communication and trust protocol, stated explicitly, would help sort out these situations. The entire team would need to buy into these behaviors and remain diligent in practicing them because they would be seen as role models for the rest of the company.

Documentation would be essential to all of their activities, especially because the information must be shared with the organization. Documentation and sharing information were also central to the process of onboarding new members and updating their leaders. For their first documentation project, the Solid Infrastructure Committee drew up an infrastructure agreement and protocol for the ROI Partners.

Like digging a foundation or hammering shingles onto a roof in the hot sun, creating a Solid Infrastructure was not glamorous or fun. But it had to be done. Like constructing a building, if the various jobs were done right, they were never given another thought. If any one of those jobs wasn't performed correctly, a catastrophe could result.

Phoenix and his committee looked around at the infrastructure they had created and saw that their work was solid.

For many years the phoenix worked hard, with the help of its friends, guiding and protecting the animals. But eventually it tired again. "I must rest now," the phoenix said. "I must not get so weary that I'm of no use to anyone. I must store up the strength to take my long journey again."

CHAPTER TWENTY-THREE

STRUCTURED RENEWAL

The principle of Structured Renewal was the last of the Phoenix Principles the ROI Partners had to put into place. It would be critical to their ongoing success. To that end, Phoenix and the Structured Renewal

THE PHOENIX PRINCIPLES
- The Best People
- Compelling Purpose
- Strategic and Measurable Actions
- Solid Infrastructure
- **Structured Renewal**

Committee, consisting of Darla, the head of Xine-Ohp's Training Department, and Keenan from sales, asked the consulting partner to attend their first meeting.

"If we don't continue to grow and have fresh ideas," Phoenix explained, after they had settled down to business, "we might become stale or stall out altogether. We can't expect to have all the answers, but the moment we think we do, not only will we cease growing ourselves, but also we won't allow others to grow either."

"If we don't grow in our experiences of inclusion, we'll be ineffective advocates for issues that don't relate to us personally," said Keenan. Because Keenan was paraplegic, he spoke from his real-life experiences. He'd had many struggles within the business community to have the chance to achieve his potential.

"That would be certain doom for the ROI Partners," Phoenix said.

Darla readily agreed with them. "As you said in the Forward, each of us is on a personal inclusion journey, and, as we continue to make progress, our individual personal growth will increase the awareness and competence of the entire team."

The consulting partner described for the committee some individual and group learning activities involving inclusion that would keep the ROI Partners interested and challenged. The committee agreed to schedule some of these activities for the ROI Partners. Some were solo activities, while others were to be done in small groups or with the entire team of ROI Partners. Some activities required deep thinking. Others were designed to have an impact on an individual's feelings. Still others were designed as interventions, if needed, to change behaviors and actions.

"As the ROI Partners continue to work together," Phoenix advised, "these renewal activities may become as important as the inclusion work itself, because part of their purpose is to stimulate new ideas and thoughts." Her knowledge came from the initial research she'd done while creating the Phoenix Principles.

After the committee tried one exercise, which was led by the consulting partner and was aimed at encouraging difficult discussions and debates, they thought it was a healthy process overall. They felt the exercise promoted an inclusive atmosphere where all ideas were welcomed.

In addition to their discussion on personal renewal by continuous learning, the committee talked about changing the composition of the ROI Partners at predetermined intervals. Phoenix wanted a structured process that assured renewal of the team by adding new blood on a regular basis. "When I first started researching this topic," Phoenix said, "I found that in some initiatives, the same people stayed involved for up to seven years or more."

"Seven years? No way!" Keenan exclaimed. Phoenix and Darla laughed because they were both thinking about the intensity of this work, which was in addition to their regular duties.

"After seven years, I think I would be very tired of the same team," Darla said. "How could you stay productive under those conditions?"

"Worse yet," Phoenix said, "others simply didn't specify the length of the service, which left both the individuals and the team open to anything."

"No one should be indefinitely appointed to any assignment," Keenan remarked.

"I agree," Phoenix said. "New people always bring new insights and approaches. Also, if the same people are on the same assignment for long periods of time, they tend to become insular. Unhealthy subcultures can form. We want to avoid that at Xine-Ohp."

"Our people are working hard on this intense assignment," Keenan said.

Darla agreed. "They need to know it won't last forever."

The committee agreed unanimously and then decided on a maximum term of two years, with one exception. Because the ROI Partners was a start-up venture, Phoenix would serve as the leader for three years; however, future leaders would serve only two years like the other team members.

When their first meeting was over, the committee members felt they had formed an excellent strategy for Structured Renewal.

Over the next few weeks, Keenan worked with Sally, an ROI Partner from HR on the Best People Committee, to develop a process that would ultimately turn over approximately 20% –25% of the ROI Partners every twelve to eighteen months, depending on projects, deliverables, and other situations. Staggering the members' terms in this way would assure the team's continuity, as well as its vitality.

Darla also worked with Sally to assist the ROI Partners in developing and administering a 360-degree performance review on each team member. This review would be conducted annually, and everyone would be required to participate. Sally suggested, and the Structured Renewal Committee agreed, that staggering the process would be more manageable, with no more than two members evaluated each month. Phoenix would meet with each of the ROI Partners individually to review the findings of the 360-degree review and develop plans to enhance any weak areas and build on strengths. The SVP of operations would administer Phoenix's review.

It was Phoenix's goal, and the Structured Renewal and Best People committees agreed it was also their goal, to make the ROI Partners assignment an excellent developmental opportunity for employees at Xine-Ohp. They reasoned that because "the best of the best" were going to be evaluated by their peers in this highly competitive corporate culture, everyone would want a stellar review; therefore, they would try harder—even though the results of the reviews were kept confidential.

At one important meeting of the Structured Renewal Committee, Phoenix, Darla, and Keenan discussed what would happen if ROI Partners were not be able to fulfill their responsibilities. It was their opinion that whether a situation was due to changing work priorities, personal situations, or even lack of interest, a ROI Partner must always be able exit with dignity. This was important to the exiting member and also to the ongoing team. If anyone left or was asked to leave, it would be done in a manner that maintained his or her personal integrity, both inside the ROI Partners and throughout the organization. Phoenix did not want her peers to feel trapped or have others accuse them of not being advocates of inclusion if they needed to quit. These things had happened in other companies. They were determined it wouldn't happen at Xine-Ohp.

Phoenix and the Structured Renewal Committee also wanted to ensure that upon leaving the ROI Partners, a member's service would be favorably recognized throughout the organization. ROI Partners were serving above and beyond the call of duty. The committee also wanted to create ways for ROI Partners to participate in the process even after they retired from the team. The committee worked with Sally and the Best People Committee and some of the other ROI Partners to create an ROI Alumni Champions Team (ROI ACT), which would be periodically invited to participate in certain activities and be kept informed of continued progress and challenges. Phoenix envisioned that, over time, these alumni would become valuable to the infrastructure of the ROI Partners.

As a result of this proactive Structured Renewal process, with its predetermined time line for members, the ROI Partners would be constantly looking for the Best People. The ROI Resource Network (those who were qualified but had been unable to serve) would become a major component of this process. In the future the Best People Committee, in conjunction with the Structured Renewal Committee, would carry out the search process that had been so time and labor intensive for Phoenix. The Best People Committee would onboard new members and assign mentors for them.

"I think we should keep this idea of an annual Forward," Keenan suggested.

"Yes," Phoenix said. "It's important to review and renew the strategies and plans on an annual basis."

Darla agreed as well. They all viewed it as a chance to review what works and take into account other best practices they would learn during the year. The Forward would set the course for the work for the upcoming year and serve to onboard new team members, or transition members to new committees or subcommittees. It would be a lot of fun, too.

Phoenix suggested to the committee that, as part of their function, they would take time at the end of each ROI Partners meeting to assess the team's progress and evaluate it against the Phoenix Principles. In this way, the ROI Partners would soon become experts on its five precepts.

With the Structured Renewal Committee dedicated to making sure that the ROI Partners were continuously challenged and renewed, all components of the Phoenix Principles were in place.

And so the phoenix sat down on its perch on the highest branch of the tallest tree. It drank thirstily from golden sunbeams and fed hungrily on the fragrant forest air until it became again the most awesome bird of the forest. It sang its sweet, melodious song to every creature that would listen.

CHAPTER TWENTY-FOUR

THE SUMMIT

The day arrived for Phoenix and his ROI Partners to present their comprehensive ROI Plan and Strategy for final approval to the Executive Leadership Team. Phoenix and two of his team waited outside the boardroom on the twenty-fifth floor. This time Phoenix was not awed by inconsequential things like expensive artwork, plush carpeting, or furniture. He did not feel the angst about presenting in this rarefied environment that he'd felt six months earlier. He was confident that his team would make millions for Xine-Ohp. In addition, he was not alone this time for the presentation and all its challenges.

The team members who had accompanied him, however, were not so confident. Keenan kept tapping his pen against the arm of his wheelchair, and Regina kept straightening her shirt collar. Though they were accomplished businesspeople, they had never before faced the entire Executive Leadership Team.

Phoenix reviewed the six months that had passed since he'd started his search and selection of the ROI Partners. He was no longer intimidated by the scope and magnitude of this assignment. He no longer considered his career threatened by the project. In fact, he relished this work. He realized now that it had been a pardon, not a death sentence. He had been given the gift of freedom to explore his potential as a leader.

But it had been tedious work. All the ROI Partners had worked hard to finalize their plans and prepare themselves to meet the Executive Leadership Team. Phoenix sank back in his chair and rested his head against the high back. "I was just thinking," he said to his companions. "We've put in the hardest work of our lives in the past few months. I'm thinking about structuring a bit of personal renewal—otherwise known as vacation. I'm exhausted."

"I hear you. Me, too," they said, almost in unison, and then laughed.

Phoenix looked over at them and realized he was no longer so concerned about his own personal achievements. He had truly become more focused and concerned about the organization and the ROI Partners. He did not need laurel wreaths adorning his cubicle to know he'd done a good job.

Phoenix had come to grips with his own personal strengths and weaknesses during this amazing, transformational process. While designing the Phoenix Principles to leverage inclusion at Xine-Ohp, he had acquired some important new skills and identified some areas in which he still needed to grow. Most importantly, he was not afraid to admit deficiencies and seek growth. He understood now, in a way he never had before, the importance of competence and commitment. He would never again underestimate the power of either, or forget that both were essential in creating that fire of enthusiasm that defined successful leaders.

The exposure to and interest from the top leaders no longer intimidated him either. He'd learned to appreciate robust dialogues and debates with different points of view. He was no longer nervous about not having all the answers. Assignments were no longer "tests," but opportunities to apply skills to achieve the desired results.

Phoenix had passed many milestones on his journey. He had learned how to build on familiarity with those around him to create comfort in the relationships, which ultimately led to trust.

He felt the results of his leadership in terms of strategy, commitment, and execution were now evident to those around him. He had become less dependent on his mentors' coaching and support. While he continued to leverage it appropriately, his relationships with them had evolved. He had, in fact, provided his mentors with advice on some of *their* projects. They had honored him by listening attentively. In fact, at the last meeting, one of them had actually volunteered to pay for *his* lunch, though he refused it. His relationships with his mentors had indeed transformed from the traditional mentoring relationship, in which knowledge and benefits flow from the mentor to the *protégé*, into one that had more reciprocal value for both parties. In addition, Phoenix had gone on to become a mentor to others.

One of the most important insights Phoenix had gained as an ROI Partner was a higher level of appreciation for the work of past diversity initiatives. He no longer saw them as failures or dysfunctional, but as building blocks on which the ROI Partners' success was constructed. The whole process was evolutionary in nature, and in the future, others might look back at his work in a similar way to reenergize their own progress. It was the natural order of things. Continuous improvement, rebirth, and renewal were part of life's processes and cycles.

Phoenix had witnessed the substantial growth of each member of the ROI Partners during the past six months, including himself. He had transformed into a leader who had more confidence, a better understanding of people and organizations like Xine-Ohp, more patience with seemingly endless paperwork and corporate processes, and more willingness to take on challenges.

Phoenix had also gained a greater understanding and appreciation of many of the behavioral norms and unwritten codes in Xine-Ohp's culture. Some were shared by most other businesses. Some were unique. Xine-Ohp was a company that valued directness and needed to connect everything to business results and ROI. Its employees liked to measure everything. They were extremely competitive and enjoyed debating and challenging everything, but they also valued trust, integrity, and flexibility. They were always overly prepared and were willing to collaborate on important business matters. Phoenix had learned from experience that, though time was a most valued commodity, his fellow employees would give him more than had been allocated if he had something worth sharing. Most important of all was the employees' belief in and support of the company's leaders. Elements of Xine-Ohp's culture were hard to balance sometimes, but those elements were the foundation of its progressive decision making. Phoenix had been able to harness these cultural norms for the benefit of the inclusion process. He had also learned the importance of presenting information in a manner consistent with those norms so the employees could "hear" him. That had been a big step in Phoenix's growth, and a necessary one.

Phoenix was reminded of an old saying that one of his mentors shared with him during the process: "An oak tree can grow only as high as the roots are deep." The ROI Partners were growing deep roots in order to bring the Phoenix Principles to life by building relationships with other departments and functions. HR, quality, legal, marketing, operations, organizational development, sales, and others had given input on the ROI Partners. The ROI Partners had partnered across the organization to leverage the principles of inclusion. In doing so, they had accomplished a company-wide transformation. The fruit of this growth was an organization that was adding new behaviors to its corporate culture—improved communication and co-creation through cross-functional collaboration. The ROI Partners' comprehensive plan, budget, estimates for return on investment, and other strategies and measures were sure signs of these new behaviors. This kind of success in cross-functional partnering would never have worked years ago.

Just before they were invited to enter the meeting, Phoenix told his team members the story of the captain who burned his ship. They'd come this far. It was time to fight for their lives.

As Phoenix and his ROI Partners entered the executive conference room, the same intense stares from the same nine pairs of eyes that Phoenix remembered met them. This time, the ROI Partners returned that intense interest.

The president opened the session with a short introduction. "Today, we will hear from the ROI Partners on our plan to increase profits for Xine-Ohp. I believe in this plan, I am supporting this process, and I am looking forward to all of us actively engaging to make it a reality."

Phoenix had developed more appreciation for the Executive Leadership Team. They had invested a substantial amount of time, energy, and resources in the ROI Partners over the past six months. As the president spoke, Phoenix realized he no longer saw the Executive Leadership Team as the "Infinite Nine," but as his "Executive Partners." In fact, he now understood the value of their diverse points of view and thinking styles.

When it was Phoenix's turn to speak, he stood up. "Thank you for the confidence you've placed in the ROI Partners to leverage inclusion to drive business results. As you know, Xine-Ohp's ROI five-year growth plan is the key to the success of our company. We're pleased today to present the ROI Partners' strategies and plans, which are tied closely with the ROI five-year growth plan. Our budgets are also included. We present these for your debate, consideration, revision, approval, and ultimate support.

"Furthermore, I'm pleased to introduce two of my team members who will deliver this compelling presentation. We believe we have the most talented and inclusive leadership team in the company." The Executive Leadership Team smiled and murmured their appreciation of Phoenix's confidence in his team. "We *know* we're committed to the success of Xine-Ohp and to building profits on behalf of our shareholders, customers, and employees."

With that, Phoenix sat down, and his team members took over. He glanced at the president and his SVP. He could see the interest in their expressions as they listened. He saw this same spark of interest in the eyes of all of the other Executive Leadership Team members, too.

This presentation, like all the others, was a tough one. The Executive Leadership Team members challenged everything, as was their way.

The SVP told Phoenix later that he questioned everything the ROI Partners presented not because he questioned the plan itself, but because he wanted the ROI Partners to own and defend the plan. The real criterion was not whether the plans were detailed exactly on paper, but whether the Best People were committed and competent to deliver the desired results. Furthermore, both the SVP and the president thought Phoenix had helped to create the most dynamic and inclusive leadership team in the organization. They were convinced that the ROI Partners were the future of the company.

As the three ROI Partners left the presentation and started to enter the elevator, Lee Song asked him, "What do you think? Did we do okay?"

Phoenix looked at his watch. "Did we start on time?"

"Yes," his partner answered.

"How long were we in there?" asked Regina.

"Two hours and ten minutes," Lee Song answered.

"Hmmm," Phoenix said. "Considering that we were scheduled for only ninety minutes, what do you think?"

Regina and Lee Song grinned at him. "We did well."

Phoenix smiled, comfortable with his role as a mentor.

Just before they pushed the button to the elevator, the SVP of operations stuck his head out the door of the conference room. He was grinning and gave Phoenix the thumbs-up signal. Phoenix returned the smile and the gesture.

As they descended in the elevator, Phoenix reminded his teammates that implementing the ROI plan would not be easy. He highlighted some of the challenges, obstacles, and roadblocks they might meet along the way. "But I'm confident in the ROI Partners," he said. "The Executive Leadership Team is confident, too."

The next evening, Phoenix met with the entire team of ROI Partners for a celebratory dinner. His mentors were there, as was Phoenix's administrative assistant. The team also invited their consulting partner. Just as the evening was about to close, the SVP of operations and the president arrived. As Phoenix was settling the bill, the president smiled and handed the waiter his credit card. "It's on me," he said.

Phoenix was proud that Xine-Ohp's top leaders were acknowledging the ROI Partners' achievement. The ROI Partners had transformed themselves from a group of talented individuals from various departments and functions in the organization into a superbly functioning team.

Phoenix had transformed himself. The ROI Partners were transforming themselves. Now, it was time to transform the company.

The years passed until the time came again for the phoenix to make the journey away from the forest for its rebirth as a new phoenix. The other birds, sensing the time was imminent, gathered around the phoenix. And so the phoenix once again spread its jeweled wings, sang its journey song, and gathered fragrant spices in its golden beak.

CHAPTER TWENTY-FIVE

REDEMPTION

Slightly more than two years had passed since Phoenix and her ROI Partners had met with the Executive Leadership Team. Phoenix was reviewing and editing the ROI Partners annual report with the SVP of operations. They named their report *Business Benefits from Inclusive Practices*. It was based on their performance toward the strategy set out in their Compelling Purpose and goals achieved through Strategic and Measurable Actions.

Business Benefits from Inclusive Practices for Xine-Ohp Internationals

---

Increase profit margins by leveraging inclusion to increase sales penetration in high-potential but overlooked markets (year one strategy)

	Year 1	Year 2	Year 3 projections
Market – increased sales, market penetration, new markets	• Overall sales increase of 17% • 12% increased penetration of domestic markets that had been previously overlooked • $2MM sales in new foreign market	• Overall sales increase of 15% • Increased penetration of domestic markets of 10% • Increase current foreign market sales	• Continue overall sales increase by 15% • Increase penetration of domestic markets of 10% • Develop 2 new foreign markets

Improve operational efficiency and enhanced customer service (year one strategy)
Improve innovation by implementing inclusive methods (year two strategy)

	Year 1	Year 2	Year 3 projections
Innovation – new products, new technology, improved quality, improved cost/unit, improved efficiency	• Quality control improved by 3% • Improved cost/unit, savings for customers by 5%	• Quality control improved by 5% • 3% savings for customers as a result of improved cost/unit • Initiated market research for new product line	• Quality control improved by 3% • Launch new product line – 10MM in sales

Improve internal environment (year one strategy)

Talent – recruiting, retention, advancement, career development	Year 1	Year 2	Year 3 projections
	• At least one diverse candidate in all slates	• At least one diverse candidate in all slates	• At least one diverse candidate in all slates
	• 10% reduction of employee turnover	• 5% reduction of employee turnover	• 5% reduction of employee turnover
	• 25% increase in diversity in management positions	• 10% increase in diversity in management positions	• 10% increase in diversity in management positions
Good Will – reduced legal exposure, increased public recognition, community participation	• Reduced legal costs by 15%	• Reduced legal costs by 10%	• Maintain reduced legal costs
	• Nominated for list of Best Places to Work or other industry recognition	• Attain list of Best Places to Work	• Attain industry recognition on basis of financial, innovation, and/or best practices for business
	• Increased supplier diversity; no cost difference, but gained two new clients	• 5% savings in supply budget	• Participate in community activities and/or funding for events for causes important to employees and community

Improve leadership competencies (year two strategy)
Facilitate the cultural integration process during mergers and acquisitions (year two strategy)

Talent – retention, efficiency, advancement, career development	Year 1	Year 2	Year 3 projections
	• N/a	• Pilot for mentoring program completed and deployed throughout with high potential employees from acquisition of new company resulting in 50% retention	• Roll out mentoring program for all high potential employees
		• Pilot teaming process for leaders and direct reports completed and rolled for leaders and direct reports in 2 divisions	• Roll out teaming process for leaders and direct reports company-wide
			• Increased advancement and retention of minority and women leaders

Integrate inclusion into corporate communications and education (year three strategy)

Values – better experience for employees and customers; enhances the other four business drivers	Year 1	Year 2	Year 3 projections
	• N/a	• Improved employee attendance by 2% • 7% increase in favorable rating son employee survey for relationship with manager • 5% reduction in attrition rate of good performers	• 10% increase in favorable ratings on employee opinion survey for inclusive values and culture • Improve employee attendance by 5% • 15% increase in favorable ratings on employee survey for relationship with manager • 10% reduction in attrition rate of good performers

Note: Some of these measures won't ever show up on the balance sheet or the company's annual report, but they're valuable nonetheless. Making Xine-Ohp a really great place to work will make it financially healthier and vice versa.

"Phoenix, I'm very pleased with these results," the SVP said.

Phoenix smiled. "The market research for the new product line is doing great," she replied. She, too, was proud of the ROI Partners and their work. How different this meeting was from the first one when the project had been handed to her.

"Who would have thought a product line could have so much universal appeal?"

"Not me, for sure, until I researched cultural preferences," Phoenix said. Several ROI subcommittees had done a phenomenal job in partnership with R&D and marketing to create the new product and market it. By next year, they expected some phenomenal sales.

"How's that new inclusive sales training program going?" asked the SVP.

"The VP of sales says the closure rates are showing a dramatic increase, and there is a direct correlation to the training. We should have a report on that at the end of next month," Phoenix answered.

As Phoenix looked over the inclusion report with the SVP, she thought of other things the ROI Partners had accomplished. Xine-Ohp had received its highest rating ever on the annual employee opinion survey for company culture and values. Xine-Ohp had been nominated by a respected publication as one of the best companies to work for. Additionally, Xine-Ohp had been recognized within the industry for their development of a *Quality + Inclusion* program.

Xine-Ohp had partnered with a recruiting organization to identify and select racial minority candidates. The retention rate for current racial minorities was increasing as a result of this partnership and a new mentoring program. Also, a new teaming process for leaders and their direct reports was dramatically improving productivity.

Other accomplishments included the successful rollout of an online interactive inclusion training program. A support group for working women was currently being discussed, along with child care and flex time for parents. A comprehensive medical program, with coverage for nontraditional life partners, was also on the docket. A new arbitration process had been favorably received by line employees. An English as a Second Language program had been launched, and classes for conversational Spanish and French were being planned.

Several benefits of the ROI Partners weren't in the Statement of Benefits, but Phoenix still counted them as her own personal measures of success. Six of the original ROI Partners, including Phoenix, were being considered for promotions. And the ROI Resource Network (a network formed from the group of candidates deemed "not ready, but perhaps in the future" and "not ready because of other commitments") had proved an invaluable resource. It was a very active and prestigious group. There were still only a few members, but they were enthusiastic. Associates all over the company vied to be in the network because they saw it as an important career-building opportunity.

As the ROI Partners continued to engage support from the Executive Leadership Team, engaging with them became much easier than it had been at first. In fact, Phoenix had been surprised when several of the Executive Leadership Team members, including one who had originally resisted her proposal, asked her to mentor them on inclusion.

The Executive Leadership Team had created an ROI Annual Award for the department or function that showed the most significant results from inclusion. It was one of the three highest awards in the company, presented by the president at the annual meeting.

The Executive Leadership Team itself had changed. When Phoenix had the occasional opportunity to speak to them, the nine pairs of eyes that focused on her belonged to more diverse group.

The president had told Phoenix he believed the ROI Partners' accomplishments were some of the most important in the company to date. "I know it hasn't been smooth sailing, though, to get the results you've achieved," he had acknowledged.

It was such an understatement that Phoenix had laughed. "We've had a lot of stops and starts; that's for sure." Some of the snags had been anticipated, certainly, but many were surprises.

For example, although they'd done their best to select the Best People, they'd had several challenges very early on. One of the ROI Partners had to be replaced because he wasn't doing his job. Occasionally Partners didn't complete tasks on time, but this one had consistently refused to accept responsibility for work assigned to him. In another instance, a new member hadn't been properly supported by his ROI Partner mentor, which had caused the new member a great deal of confusion during his orientation.

Occasionally an individual or group had challenged Phoenix personally, such as the time when, early in the process, several of the team members had questioned her authority over the project. There had been allegations accusing Phoenix of acting in a self-serving manner.

All these things had been addressed firmly and openly.

Through it all, the ROI Partners had kept their Compelling Purpose. They had been tested when a major lawsuit was filed accusing the company of racial discrimination. The ROI Partners had been asked to get involved in the mediation process. Though the ROI Partners hadn't actually accepted involvement, they advised the legal team. The ROI Partners' work had been seen as a positive on the company's part, lessening awarded damages. And again, when one of the Executive Leadership Team had made an insensitive remark, the ROI Partners were asked to get involved. In this case, the ROI Partners, again without getting sidetracked from their focus and purpose, had asked their consulting partner to provide an intervention for conflict resolution.

Situations like these could have become major diversions if the ROI Partners hadn't been careful. They had kept their focus by providing support to others as needed, while always being conscious of their long-range goals.

Overall, Strategic and Measurable Actions had been a major success. Their measurements provided them the information needed to decide to continue strategies that yielded adequate results or to scrap those that didn't. They'd had to work hard sometimes to overcome resistance to new strategies in important areas because Xine-Ohp had a change-averse culture. They'd also had some difficulty in the beginning reaching an agreement with the finance department on some of the ROI calculations and assumptions. When they had introduced the *Quality + Inclusion* training sessions, several departments refused to attend. The matter had been settled later when more cooperative departments had proven the value of the training. There had been incidents when functional partners did not provide data needed to develop a strategy. There had also been a couple of small turf wars among the ROI Partners. All in all, it had been a very human experience. No one could have predicted all that had happened. Adjustments were always needed when dealing with people.

Their Solid Infrastructure had been threatened when company-wide budget cuts forced the ROI Partners to defend their mission or be cut from the budget. Several members of the Executive Leadership Team had not initially supported their function's involvement with the ROI Partners. For a short period of time, staff support had been removed. At one point, the HR SVP had wanted to take over the operations of the ROI Partners. One team member had had difficulty with her boss, who changed his mind about letting her participate on the team. Some of the meetings had not been as productive as they could have been. Anytime anything went wrong, rumors had traveled through the corporate grapevine, oftentimes misinforming associates about the ROI Partners' work.

Structured Renewal had been threatened as well. Several learning activities had not gone well, and feelings between members had become strained at times. Strong personal opinions had led to emotionally charged discussions about race, sexual orientation, and religious differences. Several members had considered quitting because of heavy workloads. During one meeting, the competency of a team member had been questioned because of his lack of proficiency in

English, so he had stubbornly insisted that the rest of the meeting be conducted in *his* native language. One team member had wanted to extend his term on the ROI Partners beyond the two years initially set.

Because of these challenges, Phoenix was doubly proud of the ROI Partners' accomplishments. She understood now that challenges were a natural part of the evolutionary growth process for individuals, teams, and organizations. They were, in fact, wonderful opportunities to stretch, grow, learn, and practice new skills. Every challenge overcome was growth for the team. Without challenges, it would be difficult to transition into the next level. So, Phoenix learned that instead of running *from* the challenges, she should run *toward* them. Challenges lit the fires that helped new learning opportunities emerge.

Phoenix was also pleased that every team member believed in the five elements of the Phoenix Principles and was proficient in discussing them. Their meetings started and ended with a review of them. Phoenix and the team believed that by understanding and practicing these elements that were the foundation of organizing high-performing teams, they could predict behaviors and self-correct their team's performance. It was a standard that guided the ROI Partners just as the ROI five-year growth plan guided the company. In fact, one of the ROI Partners had created an online assessment to measure the success of their inclusion work and general awareness of it in the organization. They planned to use the assessment as a guide to evaluating the ROI Partners' accomplishments at regular intervals. It would become the basis for all their business decisions.

Thinking about the challenges and successes of the ROI Partners reminded Phoenix of her mentors. She still kept in close contact with the VP of sales, but last year the VP of marketing and communications had died from a heart attack. Phoenix had been stunned by his sudden death. They'd become so close over the years that he'd seemed almost like family. She'd grieved intensely and missed his friendship in the same way she missed her adoptive father. Her mentor hadn't been able to see her fulfill her objectives with the ROI Partners the same way her father hadn't seen her graduate from college. Though no goal or achievement could substitute for either of them, she regretted that neither had lived to see the success they were so much a part of. Whenever her thoughts turned toward them, Phoenix knew their spirits lived on through her. And, through her work, the legacies of both these fine men would be passed along and eventually live through someone else.

Phoenix had worked tirelessly for more than two years to deliver on her promise for the ROI Partners. She was making the company millions of dollars. It was exciting. But her energy for it was running out, and according to the Structured Renewal Plan, her days as an active ROI Partner were numbered. Her transition off the team was coming soon. New projects and new challenges stood just around the corner.

The time for her own rebirth was at hand.

The phoenix had changed from the solitary
bird it had been on its last journey. Its
friends—the eagle, the heron, the peacock, and
the pheasant—were descendants of its original
traveling companions. Now they accompanied the phoenix as it bathed in the pure
water at the top of the mountain in
preparation for its journey.

CHAPTER TWENTY-SIX

REBIRTH

In the three years Phoenix had been the leader of the ROI Partners, he'd changed in many subtle and dramatic ways. Certainly he was a more confident and effective leader. Phoenix knew he would carry forward his experiences and the lessons he'd learned from the ROI Partners to any future position or situation.

He felt an intense satisfaction in knowing that inclusion was becoming so much a part of Xine-Ohp's culture that it was rapidly becoming fully integrated into "the way they did business," rather than being an initiative or special program. The key to its success was that Phoenix and the ROI Partners had successfully tied inclusion to the company's major business goals.

And the SVP had kept his word and had recommended Phoenix for promotion. The SVP's recommendation, his experience with the ROI Partners, along with his engineering and law degrees made him a top contender for the position of VP of research and development. He'd received the promotion and would start his new role in just a few weeks. As part of his structured renewal, he was taking a few weeks off for a relaxing cruise before his new duties began.

But success in business had been only one part of Phoenix's transformation. During his time with the ROI Partners, he'd met his life partner—and rediscovered very quickly the principle of valuing differences in the most intimate aspects of his life. Being able to speak the truth with kindness, receive feedback from others, and have tough conversations were as important on a personal level as they were in business. Inclusion of his life partner's opinions, values, and customs into his own on a daily basis was hard at times, but very necessary to a successful long-term relationship.

Phoenix and his life partner sat talking one evening on the deck of the cruise ship and watching awesome the sunset. Phoenix was thinking aloud about the beginning of his journey with the ROI Partners. Phoenix's life partner had very different views about life than Phoenix did. His partner didn't believe in coincidences. While Phoenix couldn't conceive of how this could be true for everything that happened in the world, he could at least see that his professional journey and the formation of the Phoenix Principles and the ROI Partners had been driven by something within himself that he hadn't been aware of at the time—and still did not fully understand.

"Think about your childhood," his partner said to him.

Phoenix started to object, but then thought about all the foster families with whom he'd lived. He had experienced a range of attitudes from resentment and exclusion to being somewhat included in some of the foster families. It wasn't until the last family included him wholeheartedly that he'd felt like a real member of the family. Eventually, they'd adopted him. His father had been his first mentor. Phoenix had to admit that his early life did have a lot to do with his drive toward inclusion.

"And your college roommate," his partner said.

Oh, yes. Phoenix and his former roommate had almost driven each other crazy in the first few weeks because both had refused to understand and adjust to each other's ethnic and cultural differences. Once they'd made the simple agreement to accept those differences, their relationship evolved. Their truce grew into friendship. As their trust grew, they learned to appreciate each other in a new way, and eventually their diverse talents, cultures, abilities, and situations had helped widen both their lives. Best of all, Phoenix had met his life partner through his roommate.

"Remember an experience I told you about, when I was a teenager and I went overseas as an exchange student?" his partner asked. "I lived with a family who was very inclusive. They were generous with their time and resources. I didn't speak the language well, but they were patient. After a few weeks I improved enough to communicate pretty well. I still made mistakes, not only with the language but also with the culture, but they trusted me, and I trusted them, and we had each other's best interests at heart. So we all laughed about my mistakes, and I learned even more.

"A few years ago, I was assigned by my company to go to that same country to manage a product division there. I didn't have that same inclusive experience that I had had the first time I'd gone to that country as a teenager. Over the years, I hadn't spoken their language much, so I'd forgotten much of it. In this new situation, the people were not amused by my attempts to communicate with them. I had forgotten some important observances of their customs, and they took offense. They didn't see that I was making honest mistakes, or maybe they didn't care. Basically, they didn't want a foreign-born manager. Nothing personal, but I didn't fit in, and they made no attempts to be hospitable or cooperative. We got nothing done. They didn't benefit, I didn't benefit, and the company didn't benefit from that experience. It could have been so different if we had practiced inclusion."

Phoenix's partner's story gave him the same sort of frustrated feeling he'd had at the beginning of his own inclusion journey. At that time, he'd already invested two years with Xine-Ohp, and he didn't want to lose his job. More than that, he didn't want to be pushed out because he didn't "fit."

When he'd been hired at Xine-Ohp, he'd experienced a gamut of inclusive and non-inclusive attitudes. In his early days at Xine-Ohp, in marketing and communications and in sales, he'd been included. He'd been encouraged when he made mistakes. He learned from those mistakes and used them to benefit the company and increase his own knowledge. Fortunately, the good experiences had preceded a couple of assignments in finance and operations, where his performance had suffered not because of his lack of ability, but because Phoenix's personality had clashed with the reigning culture in those departments. They were more rigid about sticking to Xine-Ohp rules, policies, and norms of communication. He was constantly reminded of his differences. He felt like an outsider, and mistakes seemed to prove he was a misfit. He was not productive. His attitude had crashed hard against Xine-Ohp's rigid corporate culture and eventually put his job in jeopardy. He had been too stubborn to bend his own personal style for the benefit of his career. Only when his job was on the line did Phoenix wake up and try to find solutions.

Was it a coincidence that an opportunity presented itself just when he was ready for it? Phoenix didn't know the answer to that, but he did know that his own will and drive had combined with the SVP's circumstances and the president's push for a diversity initiative to create the right "coincidence" of a new challenge that changed him dramatically.

At the beginning of his assignment with the inclusion initiative, he'd felt something take hold in his imagination, even though he'd been discouraged by his research about diversity and inclusion. Later, through his own experiences, he began to understand that practicing inclusion wasn't just the *right* thing to do but the *best* thing to do in every situation. That idea had been born out when he'd been preparing for his first presentation with the SVP. He'd gone around to other departments at Xine-Ohp for feedback on some of his material. These interviews had given him a sense of familiarity with other departments; it was not a sense of belonging exactly, but he felt perhaps less out of place. As he built mutual confidence and trust with his associates in those other departments, he was able to let go of his worries about "fitting in."

"I did my best work when I was in an environment that allowed me to flex my own personal style. I saw the potential in myself when I was included. And then I saw the opposite of that in an environment that excluded me," Phoenix said to his life partner as the sun finally set and stars appeared in the night sky.

"There is a kind of balance needed between personal style and corporate norms," his partner commented.

"I recognize that now. My mentors encouraged me, as part of my strategy to effect change, to conform just enough to function effectively in Xine-Ohp's culture. Repressing my personal style in order to function in the corporate world was difficult. It was much easier to adapt in a culture that accepted me and expressed appreciation of my value and worth."

Phoenix was grateful to his mentors for their acceptance and guidance. Thanks to them, he'd become a change agent rather than a casualty of Xine-Ohp's culture. They had never doubted his abilities or value, only his commitment. Inclusion, as his mentors had made him understand, must be led from the heart. People can achieve amazing results despite enormous challenges if they are courageous, determined, and committed to success.

Through their encouragement, his mentors helped him understand that he did have passion for the work. At times, he'd been absolutely driven toward the success of the ROI Partners, not out of fear but out of something more he was reaching for. There was a fire inside him, perhaps a cross between empathy and anger, that made him want to change things. People spent their lives in organizations like Xine-Ohp. He wanted to create something better for all those other people who had not been given a chance to prove their talent and potential.

"I think you can accept much about Xine-Ohp now that you once resisted," said Phoenix's life partner, "because you've learned how to create change when it's needed."

"That's true," Phoenix agreed. As he said the words, he realized that his drive to establish the ROI Partners involved more than simply providing a better chance for others. He wanted to empower them to create change in their own environments.

He had grown into a real leader.

The phoenix shook itself, and as it scattered crystalline drops among its companions, it noticed what it had not noticed before. It saw the strength of the eagle, the majesty of the heron, the glory of the peacock, and the shrewdness of the pheasant. The phoenix began its song again. This time its friends joined in, and they sang their five notes in perfect harmony.

CHAPTER TWENTY-SEVEN

CELEBRATION

Tonight, the national industry awards ceremony was being held. It had been nine years since Phoenix started the ROI Partners. Xine-Ohp was going to be acknowledged by a prestigious international business magazine with one of its top awards, as a Best Practices Company for Innovative Work and Financial Success. The award would underscore a pronouncement by the investment community that Xine-Ohp was currently the most profitable organization in its industry. Phoenix was one of three distinguished people who were accepting the highly coveted award. She had been elected their spokesperson and had forty-five minutes to speak.

When her time as leader of the ROI Partners came to an end, Phoenix had remained active in the ROI Alumni Champions Team and had been pleased with the succession of leadership since that time. The ROI Partners had made phenomenal strides and by now had returned hundreds of millions of dollars to the company's shareholders.

Phoenix was now an SVP and one of twelve people who made up the Executive Leadership Team, formerly known as the "Infinite Nine." Rumor had it that they were now sometimes referred to as the "Dirty Dozen." Phoenix laughed at the thought. She'd lost the argument against nicknaming the Executive Leadership Team years ago and didn't suspect she would do any better discouraging this new nickname.

Corporate headquarters was now housed in a new building, and the executive offices, once on the twenty-fifth floor, had been moved to a smaller suite, closer to the ground, with a less ostentatious decor.

The Executive Leadership Team now breathed the same air as everyone else, and the enormous conference table was a better fit for twelve people than nine. Phoenix was pleased that another original member of the ROI Partners was also on the Executive Leadership Team. They shared fond memories of "the good old days" starting up the inclusion initiative.

The president had long since retired, taking advantage of a substantial bonus package that had, at least partially, resulted from the significant profitability and contributions of the ROI Partners. Phoenix and her former president still talked occasionally and had a standing appointment once a year. Phoenix was convinced that, as a shareholder, the former president was making sure his retirement funds were being well managed. The former president had arrived early for the awards presentation and had spoken to Phoenix briefly. He was now sitting in the front row.

The SVP of operations had left Xine-Ohp to become president of another company in a different industry. They had developed a great rapport while Phoenix was starting the ROI Partners and continued to keep in touch with each other. In fact, he had attempted to recruit Phoenix as his second in command. He'd told Phoenix countless times, "You're always looking for new challenges. This work has great interest from the top and is an opportunity of a lifetime!" Where had Phoenix heard *those* words before? She was extremely honored by her former SVP's offer but had not seriously considered making a transition. It wasn't the right opportunity for her—it didn't get her fires burning.

He was also in the audience tonight. Phoenix was honored that he'd returned from a vacation with his family two days early just to be present on this day. Phoenix smiled as she thought back to that first presentation she'd made to the Executive Leadership Team, when she felt her SVP had abandoned her because he'd left immediately after the meeting to go on vacation. Phoenix had never forgotten that incident. It had taught her a valuable lesson about trust.

Phoenix's surviving mentor, the VP of sales, had retired several years before. Though she didn't need to work, she'd opened up a small consulting practice. They remained in contact, and as life would have it, she now worked for Phoenix. Phoenix had engaged her mentor's firm to do some work for Xine-Ohp. The two of them continued to enjoy a great working relationship, as peers now instead of mentor and *protégé*. They truly lived the ideal of reciprocal value relationships. Now her former mentor and current consulting partner often picked up the checks for meals. In fact, she'd joined Phoenix the night before for dinner. They had both spoken fondly about the VP of marketing and communications.

Phoenix also stayed in contact with the consulting partner she'd used for that first Forward. She sometimes contracted her services for various other important projects beyond inclusion. They maintained a great friendship. They'd flown to this event together and sat together on the flight to catch up. Phoenix would not have predicted nine years ago that their relationship would have evolved into such a rewarding reciprocal value relationship.

Of the original ROI Partners, eleven out of thirteen had advanced their careers significantly. Only two had not done exceptionally well. Not bad, thought Phoenix. Truly, we did have the Best People. Many of them had traveled from all around the world to be with Phoenix for the awards ceremony.

As she walked onto the stage and took her seat with the others, Phoenix looked over the large audience. Five hundred pairs of eyes stared back at her. Two pairs in the second row were familiar, but she couldn't place them. They reminded her of an ancient proverb that said: "Many things may change about a person over the years, but the eyes that contain fire within will never dull."

Phoenix was introduced and took her place at the podium. She began her presentation by thanking all the people who had contributed to her personal success and the company's success. It was a long list. She acknowledged the other twelve people from the original ROI Partners team, her former president, mentor, SVP, administrative assistant, and all others who had been involved with that first initiative.

Her topic was inclusion, of course, and the five interwoven elements that formed the ROI Partners for inclusion: the Best People, Compelling Purpose, Strategic and Measurable Actions, Solid Infrastructure, and Structured Renewal. She emphasized the importance of building economic value and profits for the shareholders, customers, and employees and never losing sight of that. An inclusion initiative needed to be owned by the executive team or operations and supported by HR. She stressed the need to measure

ROI, communicate results, hold people accountable, and reward accomplishments.

"The first and most important thing," she said, "is to have the Best People involved and make sure they're committed to the project, and are competent as leaders to carry out their required duties. They must be given the authority to accomplish their tasks." She voiced this last sentence forcefully to stress its importance.

Then she talked about her own personal growth and transformation. "I was dismayed at first because I saw the challenge as a problem, but eventually I understood that it was truly the opportunity of a lifetime." She talked about the painful growth process and the need for full engagement—strategy, commitment, and execution. She described how personal and team challenges had taken her and her team to new heights. "I experienced a renaissance, a true transformation, by continuously learning from a wider variety of people." She talked about how important relationships, both formal and informal, had helped her grow. She said it was important to give back to others, to those who have helped you, and to the community.

"Never underestimate the power of diversity and inclusion to change an organization, or even a single life," she told them. "We can use these processes to change our

> PROCESSES MODIFY BEHAVIORS, AND PEOPLE HAVE THE POWER TO MODIFY THE PROCESSES.

lives because processes do modify behaviors, and people have the power to change the processes." She also talked about the importance of communicating your message in a way others can hear by taking their personalities and communication styles into account. This had been one of Phoenix's most valuable lessons.

She talked about building trust with people who were different from you. As examples of this, she recalled from her own experience important reciprocal value relationships with three people: her former mentor, her former SVP, and her long-time consulting partner. Transformation of a company or an individual is a cooperative effort, with trust as a critical component.

"I ventured into the unknown," Phoenix told them, "as everyone must at times. Occasionally we must fly through the fog. To ultimately emerge from the fog and soar above the clouds, do anything and everything you can to minimize your concerns about the unknown and then—go for it! There will be times when you won't know how things will turn out, but if you've done your best work and given your all, you'll succeed.

"Show courage in the face of adversity. Make your tough decisions. Draw that line in the sand when necessary. You'll have many "moments of truth" with yourself and with others. Do the right thing not for personal gain but to help others gain something. Do what you can for the greater good of the whole team and the organization. When you focus on others, good things will also happen to you. You won't need laurel wreaths to know you've succeeded. You'll know when you've done it right.

"What kind of legacy are you leaving in your company? Work is, like life, one big circle where things come back to you.

"Finally, I want to close by encouraging you to open yourselves to transformation. Change is a natural part of life and is essential for renewal and prosperity. Imagine the power you can ignite if you fan the fires of others' potential transformation. Go for it!"

As Phoenix sat down, the roar from the crowd sounded like thunder. She had spent slightly more than her allotted time, but the audience seemed thrilled with her message. Everyone in the room was standing. Every eye radiated energy—five hundred pairs of them.

The applause did not stop; it kept coming, wave after wave. Phoenix looked at the audience, into the faces of all the people who had been part of her own transformation. They had been there to support her as she had been there for them. It seemed overwhelmingly beautiful to Phoenix that everyone had been transformed in the process. She had delivered the presentation of a lifetime tonight. It touched something in everyone present. Truly, her involvement with the ROI Partners was bigger than the business.

In the reception line, Phoenix greeted many people who had been a part of her life and transformation—clients, partners, colleagues, and friends. She laughed with her former president who swore he was going to go right out and buy more stock in Xine-Ohp. He was followed by Phoenix's former SVP, who handed Phoenix a business card with Phoenix's own name on it, designating her as COO of his new company. Phoenix looked at the card and laughed. The man would never give up.

Phoenix stepped back for a moment to watch the crowd and showed the card to her former mentor, who laughed with her and offered to get her a cool beverage. It was then she saw the two people who had looked so familiar to her at the beginning of the presentation. The woman was her first SVP of operations, accompanied by the director Phoenix had befriended but hadn't selected for the original ROI Partner team during those first interviews.

The former director smiled at Phoenix warmly. "I was impressed with your presentation. I've been following your career, and I'm truly glad you've done so well. Phoenix, this is hard to express, but the fact that you didn't include me in the original ROI Partners team set my own transformation in motion. Your rejection actually opened doors for me I wouldn't have considered before. Perhaps sometime, if you care to know the details, I'll tell you about it."

The former SVP reached out and clasped Phoenix's hands tightly. "It's so wonderful to see you again. Congratulations! I always knew you'd do well. I had to leave Xine-Ohp unexpectedly right after I handed you that assignment because I was given a phenomenal opportunity with a competitor of Xine-Ohp, similar to the opportunity I gave you. I was impressed by that nice note you sent me, but you can understand I was under some obligation not to make contact with you at that time."

The woman took a deep breath. "Let me share the real intent of my presence here tonight. I've come to this ceremony with one purpose in mind. It has to do with my company." When she told Phoenix where she worked, Phoenix instantly recognized it as one of the most successful companies in the world. In fact, it had been for many years a consistent winner of awards from the magazine that was hosting the awards tonight. "Knowing your skills and capabilities," she said, "I want to talk to you about a CEO search we have going on. Don't answer right now. Take this." She motioned to her companion, and he placed a heavy envelope into Phoenix's hand. "Here's some information you'll need to make the decision. Consider it carefully."

That night in her hotel room Phoenix reviewed the documents. Also enclosed was a copy of the note Phoenix had sent to her nine years earlier.

Phoenix flipped through the position description, scope of duties, objectives, the company's prospectus, and its annual report. The company was one she admired, and the position was interesting—certainly it would be challenging. It was an unparalleled opportunity for which she felt a spark of interest igniting. A new challenge, a new life, a new career.

At this moment, as she had at many turning points in her life, Phoenix felt she had been most appropriately named. In truth, she had become a living symbol of transformation.

AUTHORS' NOTE:

The same kinds of experiences Phoenix had will be shared by anyone starting a diversity or inclusion initiative, or any kind of change initiative. It's not an easy job. Here are some of the lessons to remember:

- Articulate the goals for your initiative, particularly in writing, in a format consistent with your corporate culture (i.e., the way any other important assignment is done in your organization).
- Clarify the role of your initiative. Include your mission, vision, and values.
- Publish your goals.
- Identify all expectations and make sure those expectations are owned by other decision makers. To do this, you must get clarity from key decision makers as high up in your organization as possible.
- Get buy-in from top leaders as soon as possible. In an ideal world a framework would have already been set up by some of the more senior people in the organization, and the responsibility wouldn't be passed down to those with less authority. But we don't live in an ideal world, and seldom do people leading diversity or inclusion initiatives get the kind of support they should have from the beginning. Most often they receive it at some point later on.
- Understand the culture of your organization. If the culture requires you to have the CEO involved to launch a venture of this magnitude, then get that kind of involvement. If others must buy into this initiative (a sponsor, someone whose credibility can carry the weight of the initiative), then identify them early on.

- Communicate with leaders so they may engage early in the initiative to support your efforts. Show them the value of the activity or task for the future.

In summary, clarity of expectations must revolve around the scope, mission, vision, objectives, strategy, and measures of success, and you need to make sure they are realistic. Ask the right questions, talk to the right people, and frame your initiative in a similar way as other important initiatives in your company.

THE PHOENIX PRINCIPLES:

ASSESSMENT FOR ORGANIZATIONAL EFFECTIVENESS ON DIVERSITY AND INCLUSION

The following assessment contains fifty questions that Phoenix uses to measure inclusion success. Use them as a guide to evaluate your organization's diversity or inclusion accomplishments.

Section 1: Compelling Purpose

The following series of statements focuses on the alignment of your organization's current diversity and/or inclusion initiative with the organization's business objectives. Please rate each statement to the best of your knowledge.

	Don't Know	Never	Sometimes	Most of the Time	Always
1. My organization is focused on attaining a return on investment for its diversity/inclusion initiative.	○	○	○	○	○
2. My organization's vision for diversity/inclusion is shared broadly throughout the organization.	○	○	○	○	○
3. My organization keeps current on the changing demographics of the business.	○	○	○	○	○
4. In my organization, diversity/inclusion is viewed as a competitive marketplace advantage.	○	○	○	○	○
5. In my organization, diversity/inclusion is viewed as a critical and compelling mission for the organization.	○	○	○	○	○
6. My organization's diversity/inclusion initiative is aligned with the values of the organization.	○	○	○	○	○
7. In my organization, the desired end state (or outcome) of its diversity/inclusion initiative is clear.	○	○	○	○	○
8. In my organization, the business case for diversity/inclusion is fully understood by senior leadership.	○	○	○	○	○
9. In my organization, diversity/inclusion is viewed as the "right" thing to do, both morally and socially.	○	○	○	○	○
10. The scope of authority and ownership of the diversity/inclusion initiative in my organization is clear.	○	○	○	○	○

Section 2: Best People

The following series of statements focuses on those individuals, task forces, councils, departments, etc., in your organization that are charged with leading the diversity and/or inclusion initiative, referred to in this section as the "Designated Leaders." Please rate each statement to the best of your knowledge.

	Don't Know	Never	Sometimes	Most of the Time	Always
1. The Designated Leaders are high performers in my organization.	( )	( )	( )	( )	( )
2. The Designated Leaders are well respected throughout my organization.	( )	( )	( )	( )	( )
3. The Designated Leaders have influence in my organization.	( )	( )	( )	( )	( )
4. The Designated Leaders are committed to the principles and practices of diversity and inclusion.	( )	( )	( )	( )	( )
5. The Designated Leaders represent a broad and full spectrum of the many dimensions of diversity.	( )	( )	( )	( )	( )
6. The Designated Leaders address diversity in a strategic, business-oriented manner.	( )	( )	( )	( )	( )
7. The Designated Leaders are action oriented and focused on execution.	( )	( )	( )	( )	( )
8. The Designated Leaders participate in honest dialogue and constant communication about diversity and inclusion practices.	( )	( )	( )	( )	( )
9. Designated Leaders have established "reciprocal value relationships" with diverse people throughout my organization.	( )	( )	( )	( )	( )
10. Designated Leaders are being promoted/advanced in my organization.	( )	( )	( )	( )	( )

Section 3: Strategic and Measurable Actions

The following series of statements focuses on the current strategies and measurements in place to track the results and impact of your diversity and/or inclusion initiative. Please rate each statement to the best of your knowledge.

	Don't Know	Never	Sometimes	Most of the Time	Always
1. My organization has established strategic metrics for diversity/inclusion.	O	O	O	O	O
2. The strategic diversity/inclusion actions are aligned with the business priorities of the organization.	O	O	O	O	O
3. The state of diversity/inclusion is benchmarked before actions or processes are put into place.	O	O	O	O	O
4. My organization's strategic diversity/inclusion actions are focused on a critical few initiatives in order to be successful.	O	O	O	O	O
5. Diversity/inclusion metrics are treated with the same precision as other organizational measurements.	O	O	O	O	O
6. Organization-wide diversity/inclusion metrics are in place.	O	O	O	O	O
7. Department-specific diversity/inclusion metrics are in place.	O	O	O	O	O
8. Diversity/inclusion metrics are included in senior leaders' performance and bonus reviews.	O	O	O	O	O
9. Senior leaders in my organization review the diversity/inclusion results quarterly.	O	O	O	O	O
10. The diversity/inclusion metrics validate a return on investment.	O	O	O	O	O

Section 4: Solid Infrastructure

The following series of statements focuses on the current support systems that enable the success of your diversity and/or inclusion initiative. Please rate each statement to the best of your knowledge.

	Don't Know	Never	Sometimes	Most of the Time	Always
1. The leader of the diversity/inclusion team in my organization reports directly to the president, CEO, or COO.	( )	( )	( )	( )	( )
2. Adequate funding and resources have been allocated for the diversity/inclusion goals in my organization.	( )	( )	( )	( )	( )
3. A common language for diversity/inclusion is established and understood across my organization.	( )	( )	( )	( )	( )
4. The operating structure and processes of the diversity/inclusion team are aligned with my organization's corporate culture.	( )	( )	( )	( )	( )
5. Senior leaders are proactive supporters of the diversity/inclusion team and its goals.	( )	( )	( )	( )	( )
6. All levels of management participate as active supporters of my organization's diversity/inclusion team and its goals.	( )	( )	( )	( )	( )
7. The "name" of the diversity/inclusion initiative is accepted and supported by my organization's culture.	( )	( )	( )	( )	( )
8. Organizational and cultural barriers to the diversity/inclusion team and its goals have been identified and resolved.	( )	( )	( )	( )	( )
9. My organization does not tolerate offensive or prejudiced behaviors.	( )	( )	( )	( )	( )
10. The results of the diversity/inclusion goals are communicated frequently across my organization.	( )	( )	( )	( )	( )

Section 5: Structured Renewal

The following series of statements focuses on the innovativeness and vibrancy of your diversity and/or inclusion team. Please rate each statement to the best of your knowledge.

	Don't Know	Never	Sometimes	Most of the Time	Always
1. My organization's diversity/inclusion team has a mindset for continuous improvement.	○	○	○	○	○
2. Constructive and creative debate is encouraged among the members of the diversity/inclusion team.	○	○	○	○	○
3. Processes have been put in place to ensure that diversity/inclusion team members are continually growing in their knowledge and understanding of diversity and inclusion.	○	○	○	○	○
4. Diversity/inclusion team members are rotated in a structured and well-defined way to support the initiative.	○	○	○	○	○
5. Diversity/inclusion team members are personally transforming their own behaviors.	○	○	○	○	○
6. The diversity/inclusion team members have "fun" in the process of leading the organization in its diversity/inclusion goals.	○	○	○	○	○
7. Group activities are scheduled to maintain the energy and enthusiasm of the entire diversity/inclusion team.	○	○	○	○	○
8. There is a specific length of term for diversity/inclusion team members.	○	○	○	○	○
9. Performance reviews are administered to individual diversity/inclusion team members annually.	○	○	○	○	○
10. There is an "exit with dignity" process for diversity/inclusion team members who are unable to fulfill their duties.	○	○	○	○	○

ADDITIONAL

STRATEGIC QUESTIONS
The Best People

Questions to ask yourself if you are invited to join a diversity or inclusion initiative:

1. Are you a follower or leader?

2. Are you competent regarding inclusion?

3. Why were you chosen, or why have you volunteered to participate in an inclusion initiative? What unique value or perspective do you bring to an inclusion initiative?

4. Have you personally felt the effects of diversity and/or inclusion or the lack of them?

5. What fears do you have about diversity and inclusion? What do you believe are your personal risks for involvement?

6. Have you decided to commit yourself fully to inclusion? What steps will you take to move forward?

7. Do you have what it takes to see a difficult process through? Are you looking forward to the challenge—or dreading it?

8. How do others view your support of inclusion? In the past? Today? How do you feel about their opinions? Are you willing to risk security for the sake of your involvement in a diversity/inclusion initiative?

Considerations for the team in choosing and onboarding the best people for a diversity or inclusion initiative:

1. How do you identify the best people who should be involved in your initiative, and how do you recruit them? What tangible characteristics do you consider important for team members? What intangible characteristics are important? How are diversity dimensions considered?

2. What difficulties have you encountered in finding the Best People? How do you resolve them?

3. What is your process for selection? Is there a precedent already established? Who can lead it? Who makes the final decisions? Who supports the administration of the selection process? What are the time constraints for selecting the members?

4. What is your communication process for selection? What information do potential candidates need to know? Selected members? How and when do you engage candidates' bosses in the selection process?

5. How does your personal diversity lens affect your selection of candidates? How does your organization's diversity lens affect the selection of candidates?

6. How do you inform the candidates who are *not* selected? Do you have an inclusive method for rejecting candidates? How might your candidates respond to rejection? What negative consequences can you predict?

7. What is your process for developing a pipeline for future members?

8. What benefits exist for individuals participating in a diversity/inclusion initiative? What are your own private success measures?

9. What information about role clarity do you provide for team members? How are the members' performances evaluated?

10. Do your leaders support the members, the process, the team?

11. What are your objectives for the initial onboarding of your team? How do you transfer onboarding information? How do you make sure the selected individuals are bonded into a team?

12. How do you handle team members leaving or quitting?

Compelling Purpose

1. How does your organization view diversity/inclusion initiatives? How does your organization *really* feel about diversity?

2. What is your organization's rationale for a diversity/inclusion initiative? Why has diversity *really* been proposed?

3. Are you familiar with how important projects are initiated in your organization? Considering the norms of your organization, how might your diversity/inclusion strategy need to be initiated or revised?

4. What is your organization's strategic business direction?

5. What important strategies should you pursue to align your diversity/inclusion initiative with your organization's goals and mission, and keep focused on them? Which of your organization's major initiatives align with diversity/inclusion? Which do not?

6. Can you identify the stakeholders who would benefit from a diversity/inclusion initiative in your organization?

7. Why might a diversity or inclusion initiative be worth pursuing in your organization? What are the emerging issues inside your company that might be aligned with the principles of diversity and inclusion?

8. What are your organization's risks for active involvement with a diversity/inclusion initiative?

9. How clear are the terms "diversity," "inclusion," and "affinity groups"?

10. What do you need to better understand your organization's perspective on diversity, inclusion, and affinity groups?

11. Which dimensions of diversity are most important to you? To your organization?

12. Which dimensions of diversity are least important to you? To your organization?

13. Do you have a vision of your organization with all the principles of diversity and inclusion working successfully?

14. What is your personal mission for diversity and inclusion?

15. How capable are you in presenting information in different ways—based on the needs of people receiving the information?

16. Do you have an elevator speech on inclusion?

17. How important is the name of your initiative? What should you take into consideration when naming your initiative? Are there any names that are taboo? Who should be involved in the naming process? How does your organization respond to names?

18. What research have you done on diversity? What resources have you used?

19. Who might have an understanding of the scope of authority and role clarity of the diversity initiative?

20. Who might you talk with to gain additional insights? Is there a protocol?

Solid Infrastructure

1. How enlightened are your leaders on the subjects of diversity and inclusion? How do you involve them in your initiative?

2. What actions do your executive leaders take to support your diversity/inclusion initiative? What do you need from them to ensure success? Who is accountable for diversity/inclusion in your organization?

3. What are your company's norms in regard to important business assignments? How does your corporate culture respond to, resist, or embrace important company processes?

4. What barriers may exist (people, processes, behaviors) that you must consider in organizing an inclusion initiative?

5. What resources and budget are to be allocated for inclusion? Can you charge back services to other functions?

6. What other support do you need to start, stabilize, and grow your inclusion initiative? Do you need technical or administrative support, for example?

7. Describe the operating structure of your inclusion initiative. Do you have guidelines by which you conduct your meetings? What is your decision-making process? What processes ensures diverse voices will be heard and included? How do you manage and resolve conflict?

8. Does your team have any unique issues that must be resolved for them to work as a high-performing team?

9. How do you provide sufficient information about the work to the team? To the organization? What communications guidelines have you established?

10. Have you conducted research about the culture, the business objectives, the politics, and the leaders in your organization?

11. Can you take advantage of internal and external resources to provide additional insight on diversity and inclusion? Which functional departments do you need to talk to? What information do you need to review? What relationships do you have in other functions? Can you use them to create partnerships to obtain resources?

12. Do you allow others to add their unique perspectives to your work? Who serves as your mentors for the diversity initiative? Do you need consulting services? What value would affinity groups provide for your organization? For you personally?

13. How do you prepare yourself to teach others about inclusion?

14. How does your organization reward the successes of the inclusion team and its members?

15. Can you apply the Phoenix Principles to other teams and projects with which you work?

Strategic and Measurable Actions

1. How do you identify your Strategic and Measurable Actions? What actions already have been considered for diversity/inclusion in your organization? What guidelines are used to choose and implement your Strategic and Measurable Actions? What type of best practices can you adapt to your organization's initiative?

2. What method do you use to establish priorities for Strategic and Measurable Actions?

3. What other initiatives can you use for leverage?

4. Are you familiar with how important initiatives are measured, assessed, and communicated in your organization? Does your diversity/inclusion team present information in a way that is consistent with other successful initiatives in your organization?

Considering the norms of your organization, how might your diversity/inclusion measures or communications need to be revised?

5. What metrics do you use?

6. How do you benchmark your Strategic and Measurable Actions? What data do you collect? How do you collect it?

7. Do you use pilot programs with other initiatives? With diversity/inclusion initiatives?

8. How do you calculate return on investment? Who helps calculate it? Who else could help? How frequently do you calculate the return on investment for diversity/inclusion? Is this in line with the frequency of return on investment calculations for other successful initiatives?

9. What are the major time lines and milestones for your work?

10. How do you identify success? What are the critical success factors required in your organization for any successful initiative? What results are expected of the diversity initiative? Of you?

Structured Renewal

1. What is your organization's history with formal diversity initiatives? What has worked best in the past for diversity initiatives? What are the success stories?

2. If your organization has had diversity/inclusion initiatives in the past, who led them and what happened to those people? Are they still with the organization? Have they been promoted?

3. How much energy exists in the organization for your diversity/inclusion strategy, and how can you build on it? How do you maintain your momentum?

4. What have you already learned about diversity/inclusion that you consider valuable? What new skills have you learned from the strategic processes, and how will you ensure continuous improvement?

5. Do you have a comprehensive plan for cross-functional partnering? Are there other successful initiatives in your company that can share lessons for diversity and inclusion?

6. From where do you get your energy when you're frustrated? How do you handle frustration?

7. Do you know the principles of trust, trusting intention, and integrity? Are you able to implement them?

8. By what methods do you continue to grow, renew, and develop personally? As a team? In what areas do you need to stretch, grow, and learn about inclusion? What structured renewal process is in place to ensure the team's growth and learning? How do you maintain your initial passion and energy for diversity/inclusion? Do you continue to have fun?

9. What criteria do you establish for performance of your inclusion team and its individual members? How often do you assess performance of your diversity/inclusion team? Of the individual members and leaders? How do you celebrate successes?

10. What term limits have you established for members? What rituals do you observe to celebrate transitions on and off the team?

THE PHOENIX'S JOURNEY
by P.J. Forman

Long ago in a far away land, a unique and solitary bird known as the phoenix flew into the forest from the east with the early morning sun. It flapped its jewel-hued wings, scattering feathers among the trees and tinting them with a reflection of its own brilliance. The phoenix lived in this forest for many years, on the highest branch of the tallest tree, until one day it saw flames lick the horizon and a ribbon of gray smoke undulating into the sky at the very edge of the forest.

The phoenix sniffed the fragrantly burning cedar and immediately perceived that the time for its next journey had arrived. Many centuries had passed since its last journey, but the phoenix remembered it well.

Gathering up cassia twigs, frankincense, and cinnamon bark from the farthest corners of the land, the magnificent bird tucked them among its gleaming feathers and carried them back to its perch.

When the phoenix had gathered enough spices, it flew to a cliff on the edge of the mountain to bathe in the purest water that flowed from the snow on the mountain peak. As it bathed, it arched its magnificent tail across the sky and scattered iridescent droplets onto the mountainside. Then the phoenix began to sing the song of its journey, a harmony of five notes said to be sweeter and stronger than the song of any bird alive.

After the phoenix had finished its song, it flew slowly toward the south. Three hundred and sixty varieties of birds gathered to accompany it on its journey. Though it was unusually tired from gathering and bathing and singing, the phoenix was happy to be a solitary bird. It did not want the company of other birds on its journey.

The phoenix was a bird of extraordinary sight. Its sharp eyes spied some hunters. One hunter wore a robe embroidered with the colors of the phoenix's feathers. The emperor himself had joined the hunting party. "Oh!" said one of the other birds. "He knows of your flight and has decided that he will hunt you, pluck your gorgeous plumes, partake of your meat, and, thereby, live forever."

The phoenix was a gentle bird that fed only on air and harmed no other creatures. It seldom concerned itself with human affairs. But the magnificent bird, with its secrets of life and death that even the wisest of holy men had yet to learn, fascinated humans.

When they saw the hunter, the multitude of birds gathered round the phoenix. They knew they must protect it, but they did not know what to do. In their excitement they beat their wings so that a great storm of wind rose up.

The phoenix, awakened to the danger, began to sing a song so melodious and sad that the birds began to cry a great rain. The hunters were blinded by the rain of tears and could not see where to aim their deadly arrows. The phoenix then flew away in a flash of light.

The phoenix flew on, alone now, to the farthest palm tree on the edge of an uninhabited desert. At the top of the tree, it built a nest with the fragrant spices and incense that it had so carefully gathered and tucked among its brilliant feathers.

The phoenix turned its face to the sun and anointed itself with light while the sun claimed it for its own. Soon the nest ignited, and the flames rose up to the very heavens. The phoenix wept tears of balsam as it claimed its birthright.

When the flames died down, there was no sign of the phoenix. Only a pile of red ashes remained inside the nest. As the ashes cooled, they began to move, and a small, ugly worm emerged.

The worm grew into an ugly, featherless, clumsy bird, which soon grew fat on the fragrant air in the nest. It gathered up the ashes around it and stuffed them inside an egg it had fashioned from a ball of myrrh.

As the bird grew, it stretched its featherless wings. Each time it stretched, it became stronger, and its wings grew longer. It grew radiant, colorful feathers. But its attempts at flying and singing were fruitless. "I cannot fly," it screeched.

And then, one day, the phoenix saw another creature far below the palm tree. "I am lost," the creature said. "Can you help me find my way?" The phoenix looked out over the horizon and told the creature what it saw and how to proceed. "Thank you, my friend," the creature said. With that, the phoenix felt its strength return. It spread its wings and sang its beautiful song with its sweet harmony of five notes. It had grown to its former majesty and was ready to return to the forest.

The phoenix gathered the egg of myrrh and wrapped it in aromatic leaves. Then it began to fly toward the rising sun. The three hundred and sixty varieties of birds gathered round again. By this time the phoenix had become used to its solitude again and did not want the other birds to accompany it. But it remembered the emperor and his hunters and the way the birds had flapped their wings and cried to help it escape.

The three hundred and sixty varieties of birds felt the phoenix's hesitancy. Finally, the eagle, the heron, the peacock, and the pheasant delicately volunteered to accompany the young phoenix on its flight home. They would show it a secret way around the human empire.

As the phoenix flew up toward the midday sun, it became more brilliant, and its companions became more timid at the sight of his luminous body. "Do not be afraid," the phoenix told them.

As the phoenix flew into the sun, it grew larger and flew higher. Its companions became nervous, swooping lower. At last the phoenix grew so large that it blocked the sun altogether, causing a great shadow to fall on the earth. The phoenix itself appeared as a black egg ringed by fire. The other birds trembled in fear. "The phoenix has swallowed up the sun!" they exclaimed. "No!" said the phoenix. And to prove it, it flew past the sun and became the jewel-hued phoenix once again, shimmering in the dazzling light of the sun.

The phoenix returned to the forest and sat once again on its favorite branch at the top of the tallest tree in the forest. I will live again for five hundred years, the phoenix thought. I must decide what I should do with the time.

There are many animals, like the turtle and the serpent, who live close to the ground and get lost easily. There are those, like the deer and the rabbit, who must run from the hunters. With my extraordinary sight, the phoenix thought, I can be their eyes. Just thinking about it caused the phoenix to grow stronger.

Perhaps my friends—the eagle, the heron, the peacock, and the pheasant—would help me look for other creatures who have lost their way, the phoenix thought. I will ask them today.

For a long time the phoenix worked hard, with the help of friends, guiding and protecting the animals. But eventually it tired again. "I must rest now," the phoenix said. "I must not get so weary that I'm of no use to anyone. I must also store up the strength to take my long journey again in five hundred years."

And so the phoenix sat down on its perch on the highest branch of the tallest tree. It drank thirstily from golden sunbeams and fed hungrily on the fragrant forest air until it became again the most awesome bird of the forest. It sang its sweet, melodious song to every creature that would listen.

The years passed until it was time again for the phoenix to make the journey away from the forest for its rebirth as a new phoenix. The other birds, sensing the time was imminent, gathered around the phoenix. And so, the phoenix once again spread its jeweled wings, sang its journey song, and gathered fragrant spices in its golden beak.

The phoenix had changed from the solitary bird it had been on its last journey. Its friends—the eagle, the heron, the peacock, and the pheasant—were descendants of its original traveling companions. They now accompanied the phoenix as it bathed in the pure water at the top of the mountain in preparation for its journey.

The phoenix shook itself, and as it scattered crystalline drops among its companions, it noticed what it had not noticed before. It saw the strength of the eagle, the majesty of the heron, the glory of the peacock, and the shrewdness of the pheasant. The phoenix began its song again. This time its friends joined in, singing their five notes in perfect harmony.

DIVERSITY PRACTICES
THAT WORK:
The American Worker Speaks

Global Lead Management Consulting, on behalf of the National Urban League (the largest and oldest community-based organization in the United States devoted to ensuring opportunity and equality for African-Americans and all people of color) and in partnership with Gantz-Wiley Research, conducted a nationwide study of workers in the United States. Enterprise Rent-A-Car funded the project. We believe it is the most comprehensive study to date of employees' attitudes regarding programs and policies designed to foster diversity and inclusion.

A copy of the report, which was published in July 2004 and written by John C. Peoples, a managing partner of Global Lead Management Consulting, can be obtained from the NUL Web site at www.nul.org.

Mr. Peoples has committed himself to aiding companies across a variety of industries and geographies in enhancing their productivity by establishing and leveraging diversity as a source of competitive advantage. In partnership with the National Urban League, Mr. Peoples led a multidisciplined and very talented team in the design, development, and implementation of this diversity practices study.

For additional information on how you can measure employee perceptions of your company's diversity practices, contact John Peoples at 410-332-4562 or jpeoples@globallead.com or visit the Global Lead Web site at www.globallead.com.

ACKNOWLEDGMENTS
of V. Randolph Brown

Thanks to the Almighty, because I have been truly blessed with an abundant life and wonderful relationships.

Everything I've learned about life can be summed up in four truths my mother taught me: (1) God Is Good, (2) Relationships Rule, (3) Life Is Truly a Circle, and (4) You Get More When You Give More. Thank you, Mom, Arthenia "Tena" Brown, for making my brother and me tell stories as we drove back and forth across the country. Thank you to my Dad, Roosevelt Brown, for your hard work and sacrifice in making sure that two African-American boys had a much better life than the one you inherited. You served your country in Korea, Cuba, and Vietnam. You are a great role model—my hero!

Thank you, Valencia Harris-Brown, my wife, who was there for me before my business was a dream and has been there through good times and bad. To our two wonderful sons, Michael Vincent and Adam Alexander, who are my daily inspiration and my legacy for a better world. I look into the eyes of both of you and see a better tomorrow. Your love is my most treasured earthly gift.

Thank you to my brother, Mark, who also shares the writing spirit of "Tena" and was part of the original team who conceptualized this book. To all my cousins and family members, by blood and through love, with special acknowledgments to my elders: my two great aunts, Lindora Wise and Evell Harrison; my great uncle and aunt, Harold and Mary Covington; and my stepmom, Delois Brown.

A special thank you to my business partners. To Samuel E. Lynch, my lifelong role model, cousin, big brother, and business partner who spearheaded our company more than twenty-five years ago. To Dr. Janet Butler Reid, my coauthor, business partner, and "sister," who believed in me, challenged me, and continues to be my "angel" on earth. To John Peoples, who taught me and continues to teach me the art of business, finance, and discipline. To Oris Stuart, who has brought a new vision, process, and energy to our company. Thanks to all of you for your support of this project.

A special thank you to Pamelia (P.J.) Forman who has worked tirelessly on this project from start to finish. Without you, P.J., this work might never have happened, and I am forever indebted to you. Your thoughts and ideas are reflected in this work. Thanks also to those who took away from their busy work schedules to read, edit, proof, research, or comment on the many drafts and copies: Tiffany Bosse, Genevieve Buscaglia, Lynn Carlin, Dena David, Kimberly DiStefano, Angela Durham, Jessica Gilbert, Rosaleena Marcellus, Patricia Melford, Greg Pellegrini, Kim Post, Arlene Roane, Janet Stolz, and Aleshia Zoogah.

My heartfelt appreciation goes to so many friends and colleagues who supported this work. To Lisa Buchanan for her early encouragement and introduction to best-selling author Robert Shook. Robert graciously removed the mystery of book writing. To Jill Feldon LaNouette and Yvonne Wolf, who both helped me frame the original *Phoenix Principles* parable. To Ann Lazarus Barnes, Maria Campbell, David Clark, Kevin Clayton, Margot James Copeland, Chuck Hertlein, Gwen Houston, Theo Killion, Jack Kopnisky, Dr. George Manning, and Joyce Wilson-Sanford for reading and offering suggestions. To Reggie Butler, together we planted the seed to "write some books" and challenged each other to be first. To Walter and Stephanie White, my family friends, who tolerated my preoccupation with this book and read my early drafts. To Jylla Moore Foster and Linda Gill for their advice on book production and marketing. To all Global Leaders, past and present, who have worked tirelessly to transform companies and organizations by leveraging diversity and practicing inclusion.

A special acknowledgment goes to all our customers and clients, past and present. You have afforded me the great opportunity to work with you and your companies, to share and learn from you over the past twenty-five years. I am truly fortunate to have a list so long that a comprehensive acknowledgment would require the writing of another book. A special thank you to all of those with whom I work on diversity or inclusion councils, diversity departments, HR departments, and several outstanding corporate executives who served as inspiration for this work.

During this journey, I've been blessed by people who gave more than they received. I am forever in their debt and my gratitude is with them always:

Odessa Brown and the late Reverend H. Mason Brown

The late Senator William F. Bowen

Melvin O. Barber

Norman Bolds

Louise Cuyler Bowen

Ernest F. Sr. and Doris Stokes McAdams

Mom, you believed in me and said one day people would be reading a book *I* wrote. I said that if it ever happened, I would sign it as V. Randolph Brown (our little secret). I know you can get a copy in heaven!

V. Randolph Brown
Managing Partner
Global Lead Management Consulting

ACKNOWLEDGMENTS

of Janet Butler Reid

All glory to God! I thank God for all the blessings that he's provided, and I pray that he will continue to give me the wisdom and strength required to fulfill his mission for me—to help bring God's people together in greater understanding and greater grace.

To my parents, Broadus N. Butler, Ph.D., and Lillian R. Butler, M.A., and my maternal grandmother, Lillian Swann Rutherford—I deeply thank you for giving my brother and me a childhood distinguished by an extraordinary exposure to people from all over the globe, a thirst for knowledge and pursuits of the heart and mind, a deeply ingrained work ethic, a drive to understand world cultures, and the obligation to make a difference. Your love, laughter, and dedication taught us lessons that could come from no other source.

To my children, Amanda H. Reid, M.A., Ph.D., and Leon A. Reid IV, M.F.A., you are my absolute loves. There are no words to adequately express the joy you've brought into my life. You're my reason for living, and I'm deeply grateful for the blessing of being your mother. Remember the Phoenix Bird. With God's love, you will always rise!

To my brother, Bruce N. Butler, M.D., M.P.H, my sister-in-law Dolda C. Butler, and nieces Brittany N. Butler and Rachel L. Butler—thank you for your love and support. We'll always be family, and family is everything! You mean the world to me!

To my dear "brother by love" and coauthor, Vincent Brown—I knew when I met you and Sam Lynch many years ago that God had a plan for the three of us. Little did I know that the plan was to bring us together as "sister and brothers" to till and expand his garden called "Global Lead." Vincent, you have shaped so much of my outlook on life! You have challenged me and changed me. You have lifted me up and lightened my load. You have been there—showing me what you already learned and pushing me to learn new things from which we've all benefited. You've protected me and praised me. You carried me when I could not go on and pushed me when I could but thought I couldn't. You have been teacher, preacher, and inspirer. You have walked your talk. God is first in your life, and I've basked in his light shining through you. Thank you, my dear brother.

To my "brother by another mother," Samuel E. Lynch, thank you for your patience, love, and ever-positive outlook on life. You are the glue that has often held me together through the rough spots of life and profession. The love you show to all who live within your tent is so life giving! You have touched many with your wisdom, your ability to talk to everyone, and your acceptance of all diversity. You have the ability to calm my waters and help me clearly see solutions when they are not readily apparent at first glance. Thank you for being a coach, intercessor, and counselor. Thank you for extending your caring spirit to all the people in my family. Thank you for letting God guide your life and make you the man you are. I admire and revere the way you live your life.

To my "brother," John Peoples—thank you for all the structure and rigor you brought into our business and also for the love and kindness you brought into my life. Your fortitude and faith are magnificent. Your work ethic is unbeatable. Your ability to jump in and take control is admirable. John, we have had a long and blessed relationship. Again, God surprised me in what he had us do. Never did I think that the P&G mastermind that I so admired would one day become my brother and business partner. Thank you for letting God do his work through you. Also, thank you for teaching me to truly know the blessings that thinking style diversity brings into relationships. You have stimulated me, and I have grown as a result. You have caused me at times to laugh and at other times to get serious. You have broadened my views and focused my energies. Your rugged individualism, mixed with a strong sense of family, has shown me what balance can look like. You are a blessing in my life, and I thank you for that.

To my "brother," Oris Stuart—thank you for your passion for being on the cutting edge. Thank you for always looking for "next" in our products. Thank you for heading up the new frontiers of our business. Your humor, savvy, and ability to articulate complex ideas in simple fashion are admirable. You have brought patience, focus, and clarity into our business operations. I thank you for the fun times we've shared and for letting me join your loving extended family. I thank you for the many stories of the children—which you know I love to hear. Your approach to life and the love you've shown your family are powerful examples to follow. I truly appreciate the gifts from God that you've brought into my life.

To the Global Lead Village—thanks to everyone who is with us now and those who have elected to continue their journeys elsewhere. You've all been blessings in my life! Special thanks to Pamelia (P.J.) Forman for all her labor on this project! This book would not be here if P.J. were not with us. P.J., your patience, positive attitude, and can-do spirit are precious to me. You are a gift that I truly treasure. To Rose Butler, my executive assistant—thank you so very much for all you do and for your caring spirit. You are the "air traffic controller" for all the things that go on in my life, and I appreciate it! Special thanks to the Global Lead inspiration, editing, and/or proofreading crew: Tiffany Bosse, Reginald Butler, Genevieve Buscaglia, Lynn Carlin, Dena David, Kimberly DiStefano, Angela Durham, Jessica Gilbert, Rosaleena Marcellus, Patricia Melford, Greg Pellegrini, Kim Post, Arlene Roane, Janet Stolz, and Aleshia Zoogah. Special thanks to our friends in this project who provided proofing, editing, and moral support: Jill Feldon LaNouette, Yvonne Wolf, Lisa Buchanan, and Robert Shook.

Special thanks to John Pepper, former CEO of the Procter & Gamble Company. You've been my mentor, supporter, and role model! You set the foundation for all that Procter & Gamble is today—including being a clear leader in the area of diversity and inclusion. Thank you for all you've done to impact youth in Cincinnati in a positive way via creating the Cincinnati Youth Collaborative, and for making the magnificent Underground Railroad Freedom Center come to fruition through your leadership and the gifts that you and Francie graciously provided. You've been my guiding light, and I have been blessed by your presence in my life!

To Leonard Schlesinger, vice chairman and COO of Limited Brands—thank you for all your support and for your tremendous contributions to making diversity and inclusion come alive in the Limited Brands enterprise. Also, thank you for sharing critical business advice, your sharp wit, and your ability to cut to the chase! Vincent and I admire your leadership and are grateful to have walked the diversity/inclusion journey with you. We are grateful for your caring, honest, and warm friendship.

Special gratitude goes to those who have made my life richer and given me their gifts of love, wisdom, and support. I could be nothing without you! My love goes to:

Gregory Hinton

Patricia Melford

Walter and Stephanie White

Katherine and Leon Reid, Jr., Kathy Reid, Marcia Woody, and Tiffany Woody

My grandfathers, John Butler and George Rutherford, and my paternal grandmother, Mary Butler

All of my many cousins, aunts, and uncles

All of my special friends

Thanks to all our clients and friends who continue to walk with us on the diversity and inclusion journey! I admire all those who are the change agents and who are working to embed the Phoenix Principles into the cultures of their companies.

Janet Bulter Reid
Managing Partner
Global Lead Management Consulting

ABOUT THE AUTHORS

V. Randolph Brown
(a.k.a., Vincent R. Brown)

Vincent Brown is a founding partner of Global Lead Management Consulting and has twenty-five years of management consulting experience. He has served as an executive coach for hundreds of senior managers at Fortune 500 companies. Having facilitated and presented in seminars and classes for thousands of individuals, he is a seasoned diversity facilitator and training designer.

Mr. Brown has authored several other books and created innovative training activities and approaches. He is a frequent speaker on diversity and management issues.

Janet Butler Reid, Ph.D.
Dr. Janet Butler Reid is also a founding partner of Global Lead. She is a recognized leader in developing senior management diversity leadership skills and has guided significant organizational change projects with Fortune 500 companies over the past twenty years. In 2004, she served as the chair of trustees for the Greater Cincinnati Chamber of Commerce and holds board memberships, committee chairs, and leadership positions in many other community and nonprofit organizations.

Dr. Reid earned her Ph.D. in bioinorganic chemistry at Howard University, and her experience includes ten years in research, product development, and advertising with a Fortune 100 consumer products company.

COMING SOON!

INTRODUCTION TO
RECIPROCAL VALUE
RELATIONSHIPS

As the corporate world evolves further from industrial-based organizations into information and technology, the structure and dynamics of business are changing dramatically. We have at our fingertips today immediate access to information that once took a team of researchers weeks or months to gather. Young people now start their careers with a level of technological and informational expertise that is far beyond what was known to information "experts" only two generations ago.

This immediate and democratic access to information is bringing new rules and structure to the work environment. Organizations are less hierarchical, environments change with the click of a mouse, rules and policies evolve constantly, and remote relationships are commonplace.

Add to this revolution in technology and information the rapid demographic shifts that are taking place all over the world, and you have a situation that is ripe for innovation. We have a mix of several generations in the work force today and a combination of genders, cultures, races, religions, and lifestyles that make the modern business world unique in history. Certainly the world is seeing the effects of both discord and innovation. The question we must ask ourselves is, "How can we drive toward positive change and innovation rather than inviting chaos?" How do we synthesize all those perspectives into experiences that spell success for both the individuals and the organizations in which they work?

Mentoring continues to be one of the most important factors in achieving individual success. Most effective leaders point out the value of mentors throughout their careers. Minorities and women have expressed, in even more urgent terms, the need to capture a mentor to ensure success up the corporate ladder. As a result, many companies are actively involved in a variety of mentoring programs, with varying levels of success.

Nevertheless, many corporate mentoring programs are in a great deal of pain. Cost pressures and budget cuts make it harder to justify complicated, labor-intensive mentoring programs. Rather than reinvent the process, they are looking for new and more efficient ways to implement "traditional" mentoring programs. This approach is akin to fitting a square peg into a round hole. It doesn't fit. It will never fit. You can't make it fit.

Movement up the corporate ladder is very different than it once was. Traditional career paths are often nonexistent or are blurred at best. In this kind of environment, how does an individual get from here (entry level or new hire) to there (wherever s/he wants to go)? How can organizations manage talent and innovation to increase ROI?

The opportunity is ripe to create **a new paradigm for mentoring**. Move it away from the rigid, structured process it once was, back into the hands of the individuals involved in the relationships. Organizations need to become facilitators of the relationship process rather than administrators of the program. There remains an important role for those who manage the mentoring relationship process within organizations. In this new paradigm, that role is to create an environment in which individuals are encouraged to establish meaningful business relationships, and in which each individual possesses the core competencies to make these relationships happen with minimal structure and intervention by the organization.

One important ingredient in successful mentoring that structured corporate programs often miss is that the majority of the best mentoring relationships are informal. The participants have chosen each other. We call this the "heart of mentoring."

The term "heart of mentoring" is often forbidden in the corporate world. But in fact, when you ask any successful leader about some of the characteristics of his or her most treasured mentoring relationships, the "heart" factor stands out. Statements like the following are more common than not:

She cared for me.

He gave me tough feedback in a way I could hear it.

I trust him.

She was there when I needed her.

He was dedicated to my success.

We both got something out of the relationship.

It was a special relationship and didn't feel like work.

We had fun.

We stayed in touch.

We're still friends even though I left the company years ago.

Another way to say this is that the best mentoring relationships are human and personal. Though they may be founded on business, they are not cold or sterile. Their hearts beat in a human rhythm. Their connections flow with human warmth and caring.

Another important reality in mentoring is that in today's fast-flowing, information-rich, structurally evolved environment, individuals and organizations need to be able to create effective "mentoring-*type*" relationships that take into account the changing and diverse nature of that environment.

In today's business environment, it's important for individuals to recognize that they control their own careers and to take the initiative in their own career planning and development process. While they need mentors in the traditional sense, they also need a **network of relationships**. It would be wonderful if a person could identify that one perfect person who has all the answers and who could guide him or her on that journey through the corporate world. Wouldn't it be easy to relax and be pointed in the right direction and be supported along the path of success? Sorry, but that scenario is a fantasy. It's a dream that can be broken faster than you can say the word "mentor." The truth is that an individual often needs a variety of relationships over time, or even at the same time. S/he will have to consciously pursue those relationships that s/he wants to develop and become an expert at capturing the "heart" of a potential mentoring partner.

In addition, those who would be mentors need some ***reciprocal value*** on a practical level for their time and knowledge. The new requirement is that the "*protégé*" or pursuing partner needs skills or knowledge that enables him/her to provide something in return. Anyone who wants a mentoring partner must be a person someone else would want to invest in.

The new challenge for corporations is to create an environment in which **Reciprocal Value Relationships** can grow and prosper. Because it is impossible to legislate the heart, the responsibility for these relationships must shift to the individuals involved, rather than be heavily structured and directed by the organization. The individuals who want to acquire these relationships must develop the capacity and skills to capture each other's hearts in a way that creates value-added business results for themselves and for the organization as a whole.

The opportunity for the organization rests in providing basic instruction and education on creating **Reciprocal Value Relationships (RVR)**, creating a common language for communication, and providing a supportive environment in which to nurture the growth of the relationships.

This book has been designed for individuals who want to begin to establish RVR relationships with others and also for leaders who are responsible for establishing or supporting RVRs in their department, divisions, or companies. RVR can be used as a change management tool for organizations rooted in hierarchy and the traditional mentoring framework. The future belongs to those who embrace this model. Those who cast their nets widest will find success quickest.

To find out more about The Phoenix Principles or Reciprocal Value Mentoring, contact globallead@globallead.com or visit the Global Lead Management Consulting Website at www.global-lead.com.